SAND CARVING GLASS
A BEGINNER'S GUIDE

This work is dedicated with love and appreciation to my parents, Don and Edith Watson, and my wife Barbara, without whose support and understanding this book would not have been possible.

SAND CARVING GLASS
A BEGINNER'S GUIDE

L. S. WATSON

TAB Books
Division of McGraw-Hill, Inc.
Blue Ridge Summit, PA 17294-0850

FIRST EDITION
SIXTH PRINTING

© 1986 by **TAB Books**.
TAB Books is a division of McGraw-Hill, Inc.

Library of Congress Cataloging-in-Publication Data

Watson, L. S.
    Sand carving glass.

    Includes index.
    1. Sand-blast.   2. Glass engraving.   I. Title.
TP864.W38   1986   748.6   85-22276
ISBN 0-8306-0668-8
ISBN 0-8306-1668-3 (pbk.)

Front cover (clockwise from top left): ''Midnight Lotus'' paperweight. Winner of the ''Excellence in Technique in Art Glass'' award presented at the Society of Glass Decorators convention in Montreal, Quebec 1982-83. Copyright 1981 by L.S. Watson. Photograph by Bob Polzer.

Heavy plate glass kitchen door engraved and etched with motifs related to the setting. Designed and engraved by noted diamond-point engraver William Meadows of Somerset, England. Reproduced by permission of William Meadows. Photography courtesy of S.W. Kenyon, Wellington, Somerset, England.

''Hades Fire'' cameo vase designed by Yrjo Rosola of Finland and exhibited at the 1937 Paris World's Fair. Reproduced by permission of The Karhula Glass Museum, Karhula, Finland.

Heavy, apparently simple crystal vase utilizing sand-blasting to create subtle light and shadow effects on the surface. Designed by Frantisek Vizner of Prague, Czechoslovakia. Reproduced by permission of The Corning Museum of Glass.

Freestanding sculpture in greenish glass shaped by sand-blasting and hammer/chisel chipping. Designed and executed by Zdenek and Vladimir Kepka of Kostelec, Czechoslovakia. Copyright 1979. Reproduced by permission of The Corning Museum of Glass.

Contents

Acknowledgments   vii

Introduction   viii

1 History and Method of Sand Carving Glass   1

Historical Background 1
How It Is Done 7
Basic Terminology 12

2 Equipment, Supplies, and Materials   20

List 1 20
List 2 22

3 Project Introduction   37

Helpful Hints 38
A Special Note 41
Problems and Solutions 42
Comparative Designs 46

4 Beginning Projects   67

Border Motif on Flat Glass 68
Monogrammed Glassware and Decanter 74
Multilevel Engraving/Etching 86
Porcelain Plate 95

5 Suggested Designs for Your Projects   104

6 Additional Sources for Designs and Further Study   127

Camera-Ready Art   127
Stained Glass Pattern Books   128
Art Forms   129
Sources   132

7 Advanced Projects   136

Exercises for the Novice Glass Sculptor   137
Floral Motif on Flat Glass   139
High-Relief Bud Vase   144
Sculptured Porcelain Plate   150

8 Alternative Techniques   157

Screen-Printed Resists   157
Impeller Blasting   158
Pressed or Molded Glass   158
Wheel Cutting   159
Diamond-Point Engraving   159
Acid Etching   160
Acid Cream   163
Ultrasonic Engraving   163
Laser Etching   164

Appendix Sources   165

Materials to Be Decorated   165
Equipment and Supplies   166

Glossary   170

Index   179

Acknowledgments

As with any project of this kind, this book is the result of the cooperative efforts of a number of people, contributing their assistance and individual skills over a very long period of time. While some of them may imagine their contribution to be small and others may not understand at all how they contributed to this work, each has in his own way added significantly to the character of this book.

My deepest appreciation is extended to Ivan Pogue, Mike Rupp, Don Whiddon, Sakim, Charlie Meskins, Chuck's Welding, John Gondell, Kathy Koenig, Gene Spain, "Martin" of 75th St. in New York City, Alphonso and Tomas Arribas, Mike Gentes, Dale Goodman, Ray E. Norman, and Gustav Elstner, Alexander Baumgarten, Frank Child, Vic and Denise Butler, James Frazier III and Tom, Raleigh Miller, Dieter Pohl, Edith Entwistle, Bob Polzer, Jeff Cole, Steven Bach, Jim Mac-Mahon, Rade Parker, and the inimitable Mr. Bobs.

Sincere thanks also go to Charles Ruemelin of Ruemelin Manufacturing Co.; Madeleine Smith of E.D. Bullard Company; Priscilla Price of The Corning Museum of Glass; Reinhard Dallarosa of Swarovski America, Ltd.; Jack Tocker of CESKA Art Glass; Dr. E. Jandakova of the Museum of Decorative Arts, Prague, Czechoslovakia; Mrs. Inkeri Nyholm of The Karhula Glass Museum, Karhula, Finland; Gary Bridges of T.J. Murphy's; Paris Westbrook of J.J. Whispers; and Patricia Whitesides of The Toledo Museum of Art.

A special thanks is extended to Shirley Hind, photographic librarian of The Architectural Review, London, England for her thoughtful assistance and to Mr. William Meadows of Milverton, Taunton, England, for his generous contributions and assistance.

Introduction

Sand carving on glass is currently undergoing a broad-based revival on virtually every level of glass work. Hobbyists, artists, and professionals are rediscovering this nineteenth-century American contribution to the history of glass decorating. Sand carving offers one of the most accessible and artistically potent techniques for etching, engraving, and sculpturing the surface of virtually any type of glass. Because of the extreme control that can be accomplished by a skilled artist and the various sophisticated techniques that can be used in delineating designs, it would be safe to say that more designs can be executed on more shapes and sizes of glass in an efficient and artistic manner with this method than with virtually any other method. While acid etching and copper-wheel engraving have particular applications where they are the technique of choice, sand carving offers generally greater accessibility and flexibility to every level of glass decorator from the first-time hobbyist to the skilled artist or professional.

The purpose of this book is to familiarize the hobbyist and artisan with methods and techniques necessary to execute high-quality original etchings and engravings. In addition to offering a number of projects and many illustrated designs for engravings, the basics involved in translating designs into the proper format for sand carving will be described and illustrated. Additionally, sources for all necessary materials, exercises for cultivating glass-sculpturing skills, a wide variety of reference books on glass and artwork, and how to sand-carve with no sand-blasting equipment of your own are also given. All of this information should give the reader the ability to develop skill far beyond the illustrated projects.

History and Method
of Sand Carving Glass

Sand-carved glass—commonly known as sand-blasted, sand-etched, grit-etched, engraved, carved, or sculptured glass—is the technique by which any type of glass is obscured then eroded, resulting in an etching, engraving, or bas-relief sculpture. The eroding is accomplished by forcing a stream of sand or other free-flowing abrasive grit through a nozzle under air pressure at the item being decorated. Those areas not subjected to the blast remain intact, resulting in the etching of a predetermined design.

In addition to the beauty of sand-carving on glass, the value of this technique lies in the wide variety of artistic effects that can be obtained with it and its accessibility to the hobbyist or self-taught artisan.

HISTORICAL BACKGROUND

Although there is some dispute concerning the origin of sand carving, Mr. Benjamin Tilgham of Philadelphia is generally credited with the invention. In 1870, he was granted a United States patent on the process.

Within a relatively short period of time, sand carving was being utilized by many European glass centers. Between 1870 and 1940 in America, numerous patents that were granted for a wide variety of techniques and applications. Within 50 years of the granting of the first patent on the basic process, etched, carved, and sculptured glass had become a standard decorative motif throughout Western Europe and America in everything from the finest banking and dining establishments to bordellos. The most common applications in the early years involved architectural installations in the form of door lights, transoms, windows, mirrors, and store fronts (Figs. 1-1 through 1-3).

By the 1920s sand carving studios were well established in many major cities in the United States, England, and Europe. The importance and value of sand carving was recognized by the Czechoslovakian glass industry, as evidenced by its establishment of the first school devoted exclusively to teaching sand carving techniques. In Italy, sand carving was used to engrave clear glass for stained glass inlay, resulting in a dramatically new ap-

1

Fig. 1-1. Etched glass entryway of the Empire Room of the Trocadero Restaurant, London, England as it appeared in 1930. Note the two-tone effect of the etching. (Reproduced by permission of the Architectural Review, London, England.)

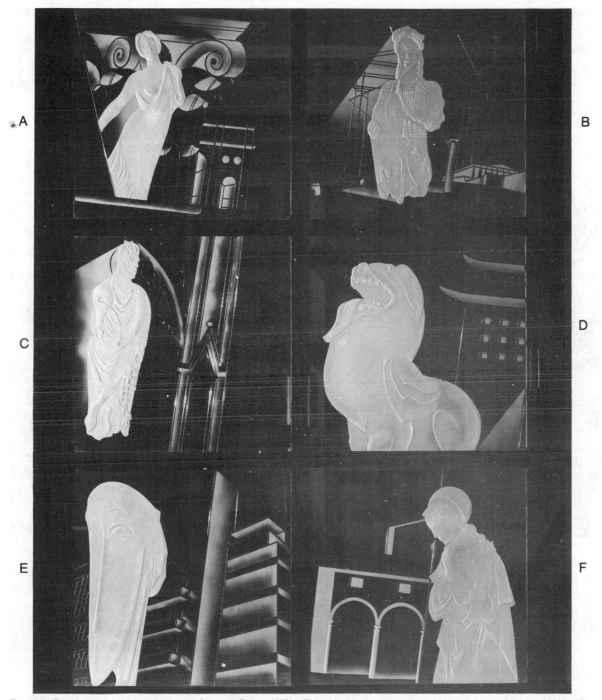

Fig. 1-2. Sand-carved door outside the Council Room of The Royal Institute of British Architects headquarters in London circa 1934. Designed by Raymond McGrath. Each of the six panels illustrates one of the six great periods of architectural design: Roman (A), Greek (B), Gothic (C), Chinese (D), Modern (E), Florentine (F). Note the skillful use of multiple effects such as shaded etching and sculptural effects within the figures. (Reproduced by permission of The Architectural Review, London, England.)

Fig. 1-3. Detail of the Greek panel (B), from Fig. 1-2 prior to installation in the Council Room door. (Reproduced by permission of The Architectural Review, London, England.)

pearance to stained glass windows because the traditional metal supports were replaced by un-etched clear glass lines. In Germany, finely mod-eled, sculptured flat glass was highly developed,

particularly for church installations. During this period further refinements were attempted with the commencement of engraving and carving decorative accessories such as bowls, plates, vases, and tabletops. A number of the art glass producers of this period, including Tiffany, Lalique, Legras & Cie, Sabino, Royal Leerdam, and numerous Czech art glass centers, set up sand carving facilities for experimentation and fabrication of sophisticated and finely wrought items. A number of independent glass artists and designers working in France and Scandinavia worked with this technique in producing one-of-a-kind art pieces, many of which were fabricated for display at the numerous International Expositions and World Fairs held during the 1920s and 1930s (Figs. 1-4, and Fig. 1-21). Many of these works now reside in glass museums throughout the world.

Fig. 1-5. Sand-carved vase entitled "The Harvest" by the Finnish sculptor Yrjo Rosola, exhibited at the 1937 Paris World's Fair. Graphically strong, this vase illustrates a number of levels of engraving and deep cutting in rendering the design. (Courtesy of the Karhula Museum of Glass, Karhula, Finland.)

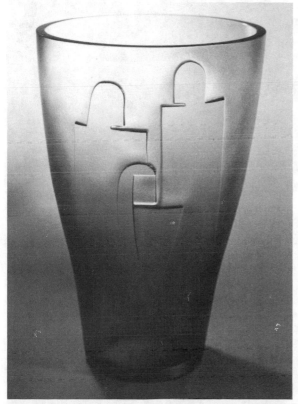

Fig. 1-4. Sand-carved vase designed by the renowned Finnish glass designer Gunnel Nyman for the 1937 Paris World's Fair. While apparently simple in appearance, the overlapping figures and controlled cutting in obtaining flat-cut surfaces indicates a very high level of skill. After carving, the entire surface of the vase was given an etched textured surface resulting in a very subtle, glowing appearance. (Copyright and courtesy of the Karhula Museum of Glass, Karhula, Finland.)

In England the Pilkington Brothers, working with the noted designers Sigmund Pollitzer, Max Ingrand, and Oliver Hill, incorporated sand-carved mirrors and tables into the most contemporary interpretations of the modern style of interior design. In the United States, the noted American glass designer Dorothy Thorpe was commissioned by Messrs. Gump of Honolulu to use this technique to design a selection of tabletops and plates illustrating the native plant life of Hawaii. In France, the work of Gaetan Jeannin and Jean Luce exemplifies this period of experimentation with sand-carved glass. Working with everything from decorative accessories to large architectural flat glass, the work of these two men should be of particular interest to the serious student of this art form.

With the decline of the art deco style and the disruption of World War II, sand carving lost much of its early appeal. Interest in the artistic potential of this technique virtually disappeared during this period and remained at a low ebb until the late 1960s or early 1970s.

Notable exceptions in America include the work of Ivan Pogue of Indianapolis, Herman Perlman of Washington, D.C., and Bob Bittner of New York City. The work of these men during the post-war years virtually saved the art of sculptured glass from dying out in this country. They worked with flat glass for a variety of applications, ranging from architectural installations to presentation

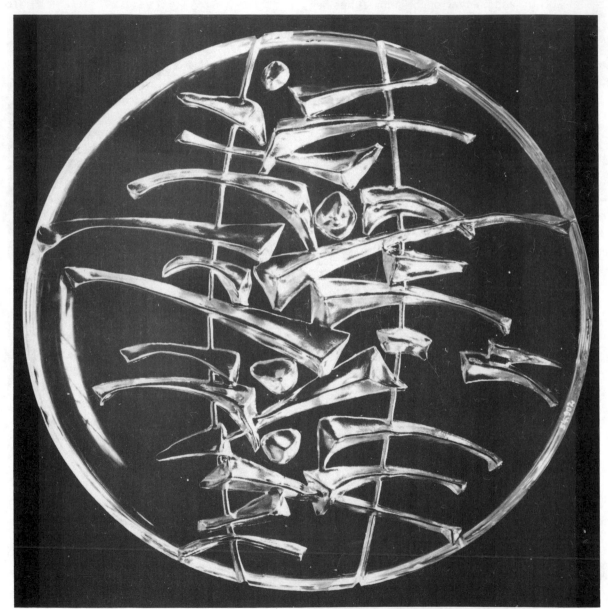

Fig. 1-6. Lead crystal plate designed by the internationally famous Czechoslovakian designer Ladislav Oliva. Very deeply cut, this heavy plate was first exhibited at the 12th Milan Triennale in 1960 and is indicative of the innovative approach of numerous Czechoslovakian glass designers to sand carving techniques. This plate was fabricated and sand-carved at the renowed Borskesklo Glassworks in Novy Bor, Czechoslovakia in 1959. (Courtesy of The Museum of Decorative Arts, Prague, Czechoslovakia.)

pieces and art glass. The work of these men illustrates the artistic and technical development of sophisticated glass sculpturing in this country.

Beginning in the 1950s, several Czechoslovakian art glass designers, exemplified by the work of Ladislav Oliva (Fig. 1-6) and the Kepka Brothers (Fig. 1-7), continued to develop the concept of this glass decorating technique. Using sand carving to demonstrate the inherent qualities of glass and crystal, they developed concepts beyond the figurative work of their predecessors. Continuing today, this work remains some of the most conceptually advanced glasswork of its kind (Fig. 1-8).

With the advent of the studio glass movement in the United States in the 1960s and 1970s and the phenomenal interest in stained glass, it is only natural that sand carving is once again gaining in popularity with hobbyists, artists, and professional glass decorators. Once again sand-carved glass is being applied to a wide variety of glass items. Etched, engraved, and carved glass is again being incorporated into many contemporary architectural installations (Figs. 1-9 through 1-12). Additionally, as a result of new proprietary techniques, higher-quality renderings are being executed on the finest full lead crystal for use as government and corporate presentation pieces, as well as commemoratives for noteworthy events of all kinds, point-of-purchase display items, collector plates, and fine cut crystal paperweights and jewelry (Figs. 1-13 through 1-18). Glass artists in America and Europe continue to experiment with sculptural techniques in creating imaginative art works combining skillful fabricating and sand carving techniques.

The current state-of-the-art is probably better than it has ever been. There are more hobbyists, artists, and professionals engraving, carving, and sculpturing a wider range of items for more varied applications than at any time in the history of this art form. The wide acceptance by the public of this work, combined with the increasing skills of glass professionals, ensures a bright future for this once neglected technique.

HOW IT IS DONE

The basic principle of sand carving glass involves subjecting exposed areas of glass to a jet stream of air and abrasive grit. The force of the abrasive hitting the surface of the glass erodes the glass surface, resulting in a predetermined design—theoretically, a very simple process.

The material which protects the glass areas which are to remain clear will vary with the type of item being decorated, the number of duplicate engravings, and the rendering of the design. The two basic types of masking formats are called *template* and *stencil*. The template is generally nonadhesive—it does not stick to the glass—is reusable and is made of metal, plastic, or any other stable material that can be rubber or vinyl coated. A piece of the template material is *relieved* of the design to be etched; that is, the design is cut out to expose those areas which delineate the design. This technique is generally used for mass production of such items as glassware, ashtrays, and plates. Most often a single template is used to ob-

Fig. 1-7 Flower, free-standing crystal sculpture, utilizing sand carving for shaping and hammer/chisel work for creating highlights. Designed and fabricated by Zdenek and Vladimir Kepka, Kostelec, Czechoslovakia. Note the extreme control of the hammer and chisel work in creating patterns on the surface of the crystal. (Reproduced by permission of Ceska Art Glass.)

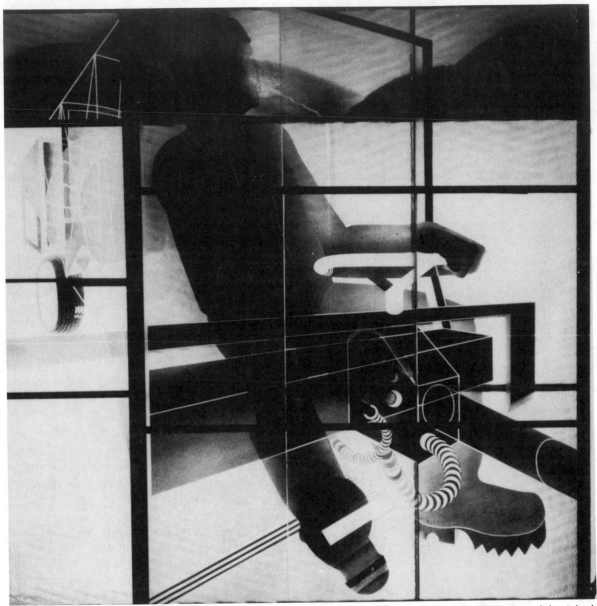

Fig. 1-8. Enameled and sand-carved flat glass screen. After enameling the black layer onto the clear glass, it is etched off to create the design. Designed and executed by Jaromir Rybak of Czechoslovakia. Mr. Rybak is a noted young designer of optically cut and sand-carved art glass. (Reproduced by permission of The Corning Museum of Glass.)

tain a design cut to one level in the glass. In more advanced applications, complex, multilevel renderings can be obtained by using a number of overlapping templates.

A *stencil*, on the other hand, is an adhesive material, most often vinyl or rubber sheet, onto which the design is placed and which is then hand-cut using a cutting blade. Once the stencil is cut, those areas that are to be etched away are removed, exposing the appropriate areas to the abrasive blast. This technique is the one used most often by hobbyists and glass artists and is illustrated in the pro-

Fig. 1-9. Sand-carved entry doors to the "Red River Saloon" of Neiman/Marcus in Dallas, Texas. This is a representative work of Glass Etch Design of Fort Worth, Texas. (Courtesy of Neiman/Marcus, Dallas, Texas.)

Fig. 1-10. Sand-carved windows of the "Red River Saloon" of Neiman/Marcus, Dallas, Texas. This type of sand-carved installation is representative of the current revival of incorporating sand-carved glass into store-front design. Glass work by Glass Etch Designs, Fort Worth, Texas. (Courtesy of Neiman/Marcus, Dallas, Texas.)

Fig. 1-11. Suspended mirror with sand-carved decoration cut through the silvering, creating a white (etched) and silver design. Glasswork by Glass Etch Designs of Fort Worth, Texas. (Courtesy of Neiman/Marcus, Dallas, Texas.)

11

Fig. 1-12. Engraved mirrored wall in the entry foyer of J. J. Whispers Restaurant. The logo design is cut into the face of the mirror, with reflected light illuminating the engraved design. (Courtesy of J. J. Whispers Restaurant, Orlando, FL.)

jects of this book.

In addition to the hand-cut stencil, there is the die-cut stencil, which is used for limited production work on smaller items such as plates, vases, bowls, hurricane lamps, and candy jars. The die-cut stencil is incised with a metal plate, thus ensuring exact duplication of the design and eliminating the work involved in cutting the stencil by hand. The use of the die-cut stencil in no way inhibits the quality of the finished work nor decreases the sculptural potential of rendering if the sand carving is executed by a skilled artisan.

Once the masking format is in place on the glass, the abrasive jet stream is aimed at the article for a predetermined time, resulting in the desired effects. This procedure can become very complex in the case of multilevel etching/engraving combinations in which the cut out parts of the stencil must be removed in a special sequence, with each section being etched, engraved, or carved in a particular way. In each of these cases, careful planning on the part of the designer is required, and if the item is being hand-carved or -sculptured, considerable skill is required on the part of the artisan operating the blasting nozzle to obtain the desired design in the glass.

BASIC TERMINOLOGY

Before I introduce projects and the various materials and equipment used in making sand-carved glass, it will be best to go over some basic terminology commonly associated with this type of work.

In creating a relief design in virtually any surface, you have only two choices as to how that design can be rendered in relation to the original surface. You can either cut into the material forming your design, in which case you have what is called an *intaglio* (pronounced in-tal-eo), or you can cut the background away, leaving your design high in relation to the original surface, in which case you have a *high-relief* rendering. Additionally, in glass,

Fig. 1-13. Crystal pyramid deeply engraved with corporate logo as a commemorative gift. This pyramid measures approximately 2 inches in each dimension. Crystal by Gustav Elstner, Kaufbeuren-Neugablonz, Western Germany. Engraved by L.S. Watson.

crystal, or any other transparent material, you can have what is termed a *reverse intaglio*. In this case the design is cut into the material, but is viewed through the glass or crystal. A majority of flat glass that is sand-carved falls into this category. The glass is blasted on one side and is viewed from the other side; that is, in reverse. This method is used often because the light-catching character of an engraving, carving, or sculpture is more obvious from the reverse angle.

One of the first questions that comes to people's minds when they are investigating the various kinds of etched and engraved glass is "What is the difference between etching, engraving, carving, and sculpturing?" Unfortunately, each of these words has been used so indiscriminately in describing the incised effects on glass that they have no specific, universally accepted meanings. This situation is further complicated by the fact that a number of different methods are commonly used in obtaining these effects. In addition to being applied to sand carving, these terms are also properly used when describing such decorative treatments of glass as acid etching, glass cutting, stone wheel engraving, copper-wheel engraving, or ultrasonic engraving. Refer to Chapter 8 for further descriptions of these techniques. With respect to sand carving, I will define them as follows.

Etching is a surface treatment only and does not indicate any depth of cut into the glass (Fig. 1-1). It may be a solid white matte surface or fade from a solid white matte to clear in a gradually decreasing density. In its most artistic application, it can take on the appearance of a finely shaded air-brush composition.

Engraving indicates enough depth of cut to be felt with the fingers, and ideally, enough depth of cut to bring some degree of form to the design (Fig. 1-13). Where an etching may have a flat appearance, an engraving would have a fullness to it, with the edge of the engraving catching the light and glowing slightly (Figs. 1-14 through 1-18).

Carving involves the sequential engraving of different sections of a design, resulting in a layered appearance, as in the carving of the feathers of a bird or the parts of a leaf. It is often referred to as *stage blasting*, although this designation could easily be confused with virtually any combination of multiple processes used to obtain complex renderings of a design.

Sculpturing is a further development of carving and generally involves the controlled shaping within some or all sections making up the total design. The result of sculpturing is a more continuous form or modeled appearance than would be obtained through carving alone (Figs. 1-2 and 1-19).

These various effects make up the vocabulary you will use in rendering virtually any design for all of your projects. Each of them is shown in the *Comparitive Design* section of Chapter 3. Following is a listing of these effects and several common combinations of them:

1) Single-level etching

Fig. 1-14. Austrian full lead crystal engraving blocks engraved as presentation commemoratives for the Louisiana World Exposition of New Orleans, 1984. The block on the left was produced in a signed, limited edition of 20 pieces and was presented to United States Senators and Representatives visiting the Exposition. The larger block on the right is engraved with a deeply cut, multilevel rendering of the elaborate ''Gate'' design. This piece was produced in a signed, limited edition of 10 pieces and was presented to visiting heads of state of countries sponsoring exhibits at the Exposition. Crystal by Riedel of Austria. (Reproduced by permission from Hausmann Jewelers, a member of the Fine Jeweler's Guild and the official supplier of commemorative gifts to the 1984 World's Fair. Engraved by L.S. Watson.)

2) Single-level engraving
   a) Single level deep-cut
3) Engraved line work, with
   a) solid etching
   b) shaded etching
4) Carving
5) Sculpturing

While this is an oversimplification of what is available from a skilled glass artist, it does give you an idea of the basic language that you will use in designing you own work. There is, of course, an infinite variety of combinations of these effects.

Going from 1 through 5, it generally can be said that, as the numbers increase, so does the skill level required to execute them. Virtually anyone can obtain very beautiful results using levels 1 through 3a on their first projects. Once you have progressed to levels 3b, 4, and 5, however, the level of difficulty increases significantly. Professional glass artists working with shaded etching, carving, and sculpturing generally find they are continually challenged in working with these advanced levels of sand carving.

A term that is invariably used to describe sand-carved glass is *deep cut*. This phrase is applied to virtually every type of item and flat glass that can be sand-carved. Thus, there is deep-cut glassware and vases, and deep-cut tabletops and any other thick flat-glass application. Obviously, the depth of

Fig. 1-15. Czechoslovakian full lead crystal ice bucket engraved as a presentation commemorative for the Louisiana World Exposition of New Orleans, 1984. The engraved design is a detailed rendering of the "Wonderwall" exhibit at the Exposition, with the Exposition logo centered between the gates. This item was produced in a signed, limited edition of 150 pieces and was presented to visiting Ministers of countries sponsoring exhibits at the Exposition. Crystal by Ceska Art Glass of Czechoslovakia. (Reproduced by permission from Hausmann Jewelers, a member of the Fine Jewelers Guild, and the official supplier of commemorative gifts to the 1984 World's Fair. Engraved by L.S. Watson.)

cut on a wine glass that could be described as deep cut, would hardly qualify as anything other than shallow engraving on a 3/4-inch-thick tabletop. Yet, deep cut is appropriate in both cases.

Current usage in the glassware trade, and most other decorative accessories allows this description to be used if there is virtually any depth to the cut. If you can feel depth by running your finger over the decoration, you have an item the manufacturer will probably describe as deep cut. This is not consistent with traditional copper-wheel engraving ter-

minology, nor its application in flat-glass sand carving, but it is accepted within the markets that utilize commercial glassware decorating services.

Within the studio sand carving trade, this term is sometimes loosely applied to any rendering that has some degree of depth of cut. Thus, what one studio calls light engraving, another may term deep cut. It has been and will continue to be impossible to apply a single standard to the use of this term. For our purposes, I would define *deep cut* as that depth to which a design can be cut without distortion of the image, and more importantly, that depth which best expresses the sculptural potential of any given design. Thus, what is deep cut for small lettering is very different than what is deep cut for a sculptured flower or other complex design motif. Only when the depth of cut is necessary for the most artistic interpretation of the design should it be considered advantageous.

In considering your sand-carved projects, there is a wide variety of materials on which you can work. There are a number of very different kinds of glass, and an almost infinite variety of shapes that are suitable for sand carving. For the most part you will have to choose between what is termed flat glass and decorative accessories.

Flat glass includes virtually any kind of glass, regardless of its constituents, that is processed into a flat form while molten. It includes all kinds of window panes, clear plate glass from 1/4 to 3/4 inch in thickness, stained glass, tempered glass, and laminated safety glass. Also included in this list are grey-, bronze-, peach-, blue-, and gold-tinted plate glass. All of these glasses are mass-produced in consistent thicknesses and are generally sold by the square foot. Many times they are cut into small shapes (except tempered and laminated safety glass), such as squares, diamonds, ovals, or circles, with a variety of decorative edge treatments such as beveling. Suppliers, listed in the Appendix or local dealers in your area can make you aware of what is available.

Tempered and laminated safety glass are two specialty glasses designed for particular kinds of installations. *Tempered glass* is either heat-treated or chemically treated to withstand severe blunt

Fig. 1-16. Austrian full lead crystal engraving block sand-carved with the logo of the Swarovski factory for use as a point-of-purchase display. Each of the three design motifs is engraved to a different depth, maximizing the light-catching characteristic of each. Engraved in an edition of 2,400 pieces by L. S. Watson. (Courtesy of Swarovski America, Ltd.)

shock without breaking. If it does break, it shatters into a large number of very small pieces, minimizing the danger inherent in large pieces of broken glass. Because of its particular properties, it is suitable for surface etching only. Cutting into tempered glass can result in a virtual explosion.

Laminated safety glass, on the other hand, is made up of two pieces of regular plate glass with a piece of soft plastic sandwiched between them. When this material breaks, all the pieces adhere to the plastic, thus avoiding the danger of falling pieces of glass. This material is suitable for engraving, carving, and sculpturing, but you must

remember that you may have less than half the overall thickness of the glass available because of the plastic sheet in the center. Careful planning is necessary when you are working with laminated safety glass if you intend to execute any deep cutting (Fig. 1-20).

Tempered glass and laminated safety glass are suggested for use in areas or applications where breakage after installation would cause injury. Such applications as sky lights, shower doors, and tables near pools are best done with these safety materials. If your installation is in a commercial building, this type of material may be required by

Fig. 1-17. Austrian full lead crystal crescent necklace pendant engraved with "Mercury" design. This pendant is approximately 1 inch in diameter.

crystal, and is the finest clear glass available. Items of full lead crystal can cost 20 to 50 times that of crystal glass items.

The addition of lead oxide to the glass batch results in matchless clarity, refractive properties, and added weight. Because of the difficulty and expense in fabricating items from this material, it is used only for the finest decorative accessories. Austrian, Czechoslovakian, Scandinavian, and French factories excel in the design and fabrication of the finest full lead crystal items.

With the basic information from this chapter you should be able to begin considering your own projects with respect to the materials and techniques you will be using. More detailed information

Fig. 1-18. Austrian Full Lead Crystal Heart necklace pendant engraved with deep cut name and double flower motif. Note the highlights on the lettering indicating deep cutting. This pendant is approximately 1 inch across.

law. You should check your local glazing laws prior to beginning any projects for commercial installations.

The term *decorative accessories* is used to describe virtually any kind of item, other than glassware that is used in interior decorating. It includes, bowls, plates, vases, boxes, decanters, and lamps. These items come in a variety of clear glasses which vary in the constituents used in making the glass batch.

The term *crystal glass* is used to describe virtually any kind of clear glass used in making these items. *Lead crystal* is material that has had some amount of lead oxide (PbO) added to the glass batch. More than 24 percent (PbO) is termed *full lead*

Fig. 1-19. Sun face sculptured into 1/2-inch plate glass. Note the form given to the forehead, cheeks, and chin. This is an example of sculptural form being controlled within a single continuous area of a design. The face measures approximately 7 inches in diameter, with the overall diameter of the sun rays being 14 inches. Sculptured by L. S. Watson and copyright by the artist.

Fig. 1-20. Sand-carved entry doors to T. J. Murphy's Restaurant. Deep-cut and etched on laminated safety glass, these doors allow for a degree of both visibility and privacy, combined with the safety of laminated glass. The lettering is deep-cut, as is the border between the clear center area and the surrounding etched area. (Courtesy of T. J. Murphy's Restaurant, Orlando, Fl.)

Fig. 1-21. Lead Crystal Flat Bowl, designed by the noted Dutch designer Andreas Copier for the Royal Leerdarn Glassworks. Designed for and exhibited at the 1939 World's Fair in New York City. Measuring just over 20 inches in diameter, this is a rare example of sophisticated etching and sculptural techniques being incorporated into a design for this type of item. Note the use of deep-cutting (the whitest parts of the design) used in association with shaded etching in giving the design sculptural complexity and in suggesting the relative positions of the characters within the design. Gift of Edward Drummond Libbey to The Toledo Museum of Art. Reproduced by permission of The Toledo Museum of Art.

is contained in the following chapters. Sources for all materials, detailed photographs of the various styles of renderings, and many designs that you can trace and use in creating your own one-of-a-kind projects are discussed. Regardless of your experience in art or glass or the fact that you do not own the special equipment used in sand carving, you will be able to create many attractive projects based on this information. Also, enough technical information is illustrated in the advanced projects to allow you to develop your skill to any level you choose.

2

Equipment, Supplies, and Materials

In this chapter I have put together two lists of the materials you will need to make your own original sand-carved projects (see Table 2-1). The first list is for hobbyists and other occasional glass artists. The second list is more thorough and is designed for the person who wishes to set up his own sand carving studio and make projects on a regular basis. If you anticipate purchasing any of the specialized equipment necessary for sand carving, I strongly recommend that you read this entire chapter, since I have tried to include information that will be helpful to you in determining what type of equipment to buy.

The descriptions of the materials should make you aware of the choices you have available, particularly for stencil materials, compressors, and sand-blast generators. I have gone into some detail concerning these items so that you will have a basic knowledge of the decisions you will have to make when you are discussing the purchase of these materials with suppliers. In this way you can make informed decisions based on your particular needs.

Sources for all of the materials listed are con-

tained in the Appendix. I have noted sources for all levels of glass decorators, from the first-time hobbyist to the beginning professional sand carver or glass artist.

LIST 1

Material To Be Decorated. The available materials are float plate glass (1/4, 3/8, 1/2, and 3/4 inch in thickness) and tempered or laminated safety glass. Decorative accessories such as vases, bowls, decanters, carafes, and plates are also suitable. Specialty glasses, such as beveled flat glass, tinted colored flat glasses, flashed stained glass, and borosilicate laboratory crystal can also be used. I suggest that you read the introductory sections in Chapter 1 covering these various materials prior to making your final choice.

Stencil Material. When you are using a hand-cut stencil, you can get away with using such things as duct tape and contact paper. However, the difficulty of applying these materials to your glass and the fact they were not designed for abrasive-blast resistance does not make them the

Table 2-1. Equipment and Supply Lists.

List 1
A) Material to be decorated.
B) Stencil material.
C) Cutting blades with handle.
D) Tracing paper and tape.
E) Burnishing tool.
F) Glass cleaner.
G) Clean towel or rag.
H) Soft lead pencil.
I) Design.

List 2
A) Blasting room equipment.

  1) Compressor.
    a) Compressor.
    b) Compressor motor.
    c) Pressure tank.

  2) Sand-blast generator.
    a) Pressure-pot.
    b) Syphon, gravity feed.
    c) Spray gun, syphon.

  3) Pressure regulators.

  4) Water and oil filters.

  5) Air lines.

  6) Exhaust fan.

  7) Dust collector.

  8) Abrasives.

  9) Blasting nozzles.

B) Protective clothing.

  1) Protective head gear.

    a) Air-fed helmet/suit
    1) Air pump (optional)
    2) Air line filter.

    b) Canvas blasting hood.
    1) Respirator mask with removable filters.

  2) Clothing.
    a) Blasting suit or old clothing.
    b) Protective gloves.

C) Assorted materials.

  1) Straight edges.
  2) Steel measuring tapes.
  3) Large flat tables.
  4) Glass racks.
  5) Lighting.
  6) Opaque projector.
  7) Overhead projector.
  8) Pantograph (optional)
  9) Design reference materials.

materials of choice. Commercially available stencils, marketed as being specifically formulated as *sand-blast resists* are generally worth the cost in the time and effort saved in using them and the quality of the resulting work. The most common hand-cut stencil materials are Continental No. 111, known as "Buttercut" and 3-M Scotch Stencil No. 507 or 508, known for its distinctive "Eye-ease" green color. A number of other high-quality materials have come into the market, including 3-M Scotch No. 300 and No. 280 and American Tape's No. 4000. Some independent suppliers of stained glass supplies and monument materials are also marketing their own brands of hand-cut stencil materials.

Virtually any of these materials will give very good results in obtaining high-quality etchings, engravings, carvings, and sculptures. However, they will vary in price and some physical characteristics, such as thickness and adhesion to the glass and suitability in holding fine details under heavy blasting. For these reasons, virtually every professional develops an affinity for one material or another. For the hobbyist, artist, or other occasional user, any of these materials would offer the best opportunity to work with quality materials.

A selection of stencils are available from monument supply companies, such as the Ruemelin distributors listed in the Appendix, in Chapter 11 and many stained glass supply houses. These suppliers will sell this material by the roll, which is a minimum of 10 yards in length and will range from 12 3/4 to over 30 inches in width. Small quantities should be available from local monument makers or stained glass retailers who may sell the material by the square foot to hobbyists and other occasional users.

Cutting Blades with Handle. While virtually any commercially available blades will do, many artisans prefer the X-Acto #11 or similarly shaped blade. It is a good idea to have a number of blades on hand when you are starting a project, so fresh blades can be used for cutting your stencil, resulting in ease of cutting and clean, sharp cuts in your stencil design.

Tracing Paper and Tape. Although any quality may be satisfactory, you will find the better qualities that last longer and do not tear to be worth the cost. If practical, use a high grade of vellum, since it stands up very well to repeated burnishings. Tape is used to hold your pencil tracing in place while you are burnishing it onto your stencil. Virtually any tape will do and common masking tape is the most popular.

Burnishing Tool. A burnishing tool is used for two very different purposes in preparing your project. First of all it will be used to rub the stencil material onto the glass, ensuring good adhesion. As shown in the beginning projects in Chapter 4, this step is easily accomplished using the bottom of a small glass, with wax paper placed between the glass and the stencil material.

The second need for burnishing comes when the traced pencil design is to be transferred to the stencil. The penciled side of the tracing paper is placed onto the stencil and taped in place, and the design is then burnished onto the stencil. The handle of a pair of scissors or the bottom of a glass is ideal for this purpose.

If you are going to burnish on a regular basis, you should purchase a *brayer*. This tool consists of a wooden handle with a wooden or rubber roller. During the application of the stencil to the glass, the roller is moved back and forth as the stencil is applied, resulting in good adhesion. A brayer can also be used to burnish your design onto the stencil, although scissor handles or the bottoms of glasses are preferred by some.

Glass Cleaner. Because some commercial cleaners leave a slight residue on the glass surface, which may inhibit adhesion of the stencil, I recommend you use a mix of 30 percent denatured alcohol and 70 percent water. Simply spray and towel dry.

Clean Towel or Rag. Because it is impossible to properly clean glass with a dirty cloth, always use a clean one.

Soft Lead Pencil. Using soft lead makes burnishing easier and ensures not only that you will get a good transfer to your stencil, but that you should get repeated applications from a single tracing of your design.

Design. The design will be based on your own ideas and sketches or can be taken from the design section of Chapter 5 or any of the many suggested sources for designs in Chapter 6.

LIST 2

This list contains equipment that more advanced artists may desire to purchase.

Blasting Room Equipment

If you anticipate sand carving on a regular basis, you have a number of alternatives in establishing an area reserved for this purpose. You can set aside a separate room with proper ventilation for sand blasting, or you can build or purchase a miniature sand-blasting room, commonly known as *sand-blasting cabinet* because of its size (Fig. 2-1). This unit incorporates all of the features of a sand-blasting room, in that the abrasive dusts are controlled and removed from the area where the blasting is taking place. These units are particularly useful for studios with limited space, those that will be used for smaller items, and arts and crafts schools or glass departments at the college level.

An alternative for the larger commercial sand carving company would be the very sophisticated steel-constructed sand-blast room, incorporating abrasive retrieval and recycling dust collection and blasting operations in a very compact area, although considerably larger than the cabinet-sized units just mentioned. (See Fig. 2-2.) This type of unit is one of the more common ways of maximizing production capabilities for architectural flat glass. These units are available with automatic equipment that moves the blasting nozzle in a back and forth motion across the glass being decorated, so that the glass need only be placed inside the room and the mechanism turned on for a predetermined time, for perfect, even deep cutting to be accomplished. These totally self-contained units represent the current state of the art in production equipment of commercial etching and deep cutting.

Compressor. It is important to understand that what is generally termed a compressor is actually at least three separate units that can be purchased individually or together. First you have the actual compressor, also known as the *air pump* or

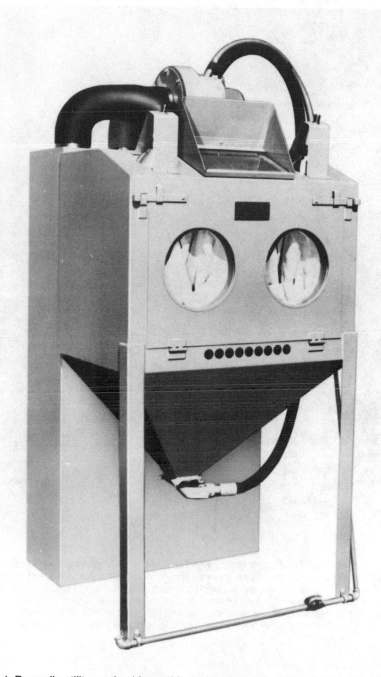

Fig. 2-1. 20- x -30-inch Ruemelin utility suction blast cabinet with integral dust filter, fan, and motor. This type of unit is suitable for working on smaller pieces of flat glass, glassware, and other decorative accessories, particularly if you have limited space and cannot set up a separate blasting room. The sand carver stand with both arms reaching into the cabinet through the large round openings on the front, while viewing the work through the window on the top of the unit. This type of unit is excellent for controlling the abrasive dusts that are generated during sand carving. (Courtesy of Ruemelin Manufacturing Company.)

Fig. 2-2. Ruemelin compact industrial blast room facility with Ruemelin wide blast curtain with inspection door, Ruemelin steel blast room, Ruemelin abrasive elevator with abrasive-cleaning rotary screen and storage tank, Ruemelin ASME direct pressure 750 lb. "Master" abrasive blast generator with electric remote control and safety foot switch. This facility would also incorporate a Ruemelin assembled dust filter with fan and motor, although these items are not shown here. This is an example of a state-of-the-art commercial sand-blasting set up. It incorporates a high degree of safety for the operator, mechanical efficiency, and production capabilities in producing sand-carved glass. (Courtesy of Reumelin Manufacturing Company.)

compressor head, which is little more than a cylinder configuration that compresses the air and forces it into a holding tank. This tank is known as the *pressure tank*. The compressor is powered by the third part of the unit, the *motor*. These parts are available from industrial equipment suppliers or used equipment dealers. It is not uncommon to come across a compressor and pressure tank less the motor. Often considerable money can be saved by shopping around for a rebuilt compressor and pressure tank, and adding a brand new motor to power the unit. I saved over $4000 dollars this way, and have had a trouble-free unit for years.

The question most often asked with regard to purchasing a compressor, is "What horsepower should I get?" Although the horsepower of a compressor is an important characteristic it is not the decisive one. The more significant measure is the compressor's *free air cubic feet per minute* (free air cfm or simply cfm). This term refers to the cubic feet of air delivered into the atmosphere by the compressor at a particular pressure. Thus a compressor may deliver 15.5 cfm at 100 psi (pounds per square inch—the standard measure of air pressure).

Another measure of a compressor's ability to move air is called *displacement cfm,* and should not be confused with Free Air cfm. The displacement cfm is a figure calculated by multiplying the volume of the cylinders of the compressor by the pump speed measured in rpms (Revolutions per Minute).

Both of these figures are furnished by the compressor manufacturer. The more significant measure is the free air cfm with regard to sand carving. When you are reading a chart showing the comparative information on compressors, you must be sure not to confuse these two figures, because displacement cfm is usually higher than free air cfm, and confusion can result in the purchase of an inadequate unit.

Because free air cfm is always related to pressure—it is stated as being a certain amount of air delivered at a certain specific pressure—it is important that you compare like pressures for the cfm rating when you are comparing compressors. Thus, if one compressor's rating is stated at 60 psi, it can only be compared with other compressors also rated at 60 psi. As a general rule, as horsepower increases, free air cfm increases. This is true because a larger motor can be used to power larger cylinders, which in turn deliver more cfm.

For sand carving glass, free air cfm is the significant and overriding measure of a compressor's suitability for a particular application. You must match the air required to supply your sandblast generator (usually a pressure pot, in commercial operations), air-fed hood (unless a separate air pump is used for this purpose), and any other pneumatically powered tools or accessories with the compressor's ability to deliver air. Thus by adding up the requirements of your equipment, you can determine the size compressor you will need. Most sand carvers use a 3 to 10 horsepower compressor per pressure-pot for their work.

In addition to the cfm and horsepower of a compressor, there are a number of other features and characteristics of which you should be aware. In most cases you will have to choose between two or three alternatives.

First of all, there are two basic types of cylinder compressors, known as single stage and double stage. A *single-stage compressor* has one or more cylinders discharging air directly into the pressure tank. These are used most often when the operating pressure of the equipment being supplied with air is less than 100 psi. Because most sand carving of glass is done below 100 psi, this type of compressor is a common choice.

Double-stage compressors have two or more cylinders connected in a series. The first cylinder compresses air into the second cylinder, which then compresses it further and feeds it into the pressure tank. These are used when operating pressures in the 100 to 175 psi range are used. Even though sand carving is not done at these high pressures, this type of compressor is utilized when a single compressor is used to supply more than one pressure-pot at a time. Some equipment dealers recommend using a double-stage compressor no matter what pressures you are working with, because the work of compressing the air is divided between the cylinders, thus lessening the strain put on each individual cylinder.

If you purchase a double-stage compressor, you will want to make sure it has an *intercooler,* which is a length of tubing, often with fins, connecting the low-pressure cylinder and high-pressure cylinder, through which the air forced between cylinders must pass. The intercooler acts to dissipate some of the heat generated during compression, and improves the performance and life of your compressor.

You will also have to choose one of three types of switches used to activate the motor powering your compressor. A *pressure switch control* starts and stops the motor as pressure falls and rises in the pressure tank. Thus it can be set to start when the pressure gets below predetermined point and shut off when the pressure in the tank rises to a predetermined point. For example, you may set your switch to come on when the pressure in the tank gets down to 80 psi and shut off when it gets up to 120 psi. If the maximum usage of your compressor is less than 50 percent of its capacity, this type of switch is recommended.

The second type of switch is the *constant speed control*. This switch keeps the compressor running at all times during operation, and releases excess pressure from the tank automatically during use. Thus, this switch may be set to release all pressure in excess of 100 psi from your pressure tank, while running continuously during use. If your air usage is above 50 percent fo the compressor's capacity, this type of switch is recommended.

The third type of switch is called a *dual control* and incorporates the features of both previously mentioned switches. If you are unsure of which switch to use or your application varies, this switch allows for the most efficient running of your compressor for each situation. This switch would be useful if you sometimes decorate glassware at low pressures, thus using less than 50 percent of your compressor's capacity, and also sometimes want to deep-cut line work at higher pressures, thus using the full capacity of your compressor. This switch allows you to choose the switching mode most efficient for each particular job.

In selecting the motor for your compressor, you will come across *single phase* and *triple phase* electrical motors. These terms are not to be confused with single stage and double stage compressors. Single phase and triple phase refers to the type of electrical current used to power the motor.

Until you get to 5 horsepower (hp), you probably will not have a choice; your motor will be single phase. Once you get to the 5 hp threshold, you will be given a choice. Triple-phase current is used for all heavy electrical motors since it requires 30 to 50 percent less power than a comparably sized single-phase unit, and tends to give longer, more reliable service. If you are not going to be using the equipment for a good part of the day on a consistent basis, you may not want to pay the additional wiring and installation fees charged by utility companies for starting service on the special triple-phase lines. The triple-phase alternative is one you should be aware of, but need only consider if you are going into a commercial operation with compressors of 10 hp or larger. If this seems like a good choice for your situation, I recommend that you ask your local utility company about the additional charges prior to purchasing a triple-phase unit.

If you are looking at used equipment and the equipment dealer tells you he has just the compressor for you, then adds that it has a special motor which uses significantly less power than other units, be aware that he may be selling you a triple-phase motor, for which you may not have power service in your area.

With this basic information in mind when you start shopping for a compressor, you should have no trouble in determining which unit is best suited for your purposes. The most significant factor is to make sure that your compressor selection will deliver enough free air cfm for all of your anticipated needs. It is far better to buy a compressor that is 20 to 30 percent larger than you think you will need then to buy one that performs exactly at your anticipated requirements and discover it is inadequate.

Sand-Blast Generators. The sand-blast generator is the piece of equipment that holds the abrasive grit used in blasting and feeds it into the air line from the compressor, resulting in an abrasive blast coming out of the nozzle. The two basic types of sand-blast generators are the open-hopper, syphon type (Fig. 2-3) and the pressure-pot type (Fig. 2-4). A third type, similar in appearance to a spray paint gun, is also available from department stores, hardware stores, and other general supply companies which do not supply the sand carving trade with professional equipment.

The syphon type consists of an open hopper which is used to hold the abrasive, a sand-feed hose, an air-feed hose, and a nozzle or gun-style sprayer handle. As compressed air rushes past the sand-feed hose leading from the hopper to the nozzle or

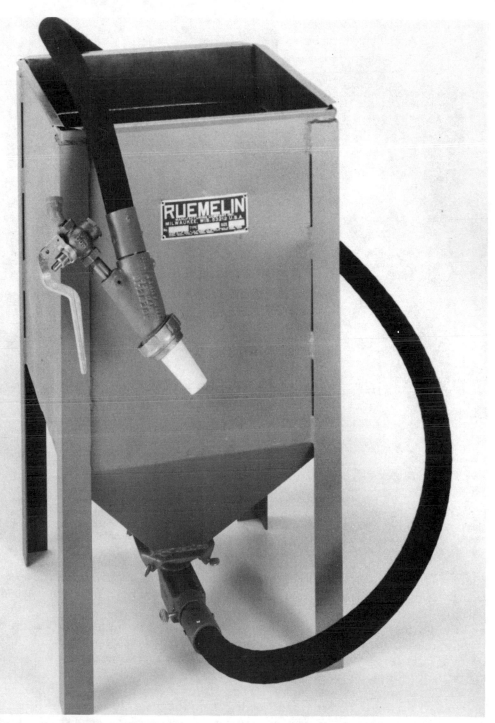

Fig. 2-3. Ruemelin midget suction blast gun with hose and abrasive hopper. This is an example of a syphon-feed or gravity-feed sand-blast generator. This type of unit is excellent for the beginning glass artist or other occasional sand carver. (Courtesy of Ruemelin Manufacturing Company.)

Fig. 2-4. Group shot of Ruemelin ASME direct pressure abrasive blast generators. Individual glass artists and stained glass studios working with sand carving will generally find the 25 lb., 50 lb., or 150 lb. capacity units best suited for their needs, while production studios will find the added efficiency of the larger units advantageous. (Courtesy of Ruemelin Manufacturing Company.)

gun, a vacuum is created, which draws the sand from the hopper into the gun and out onto the work being decorated. The amount of abrasive falling into the air line is a result of this vacuum and gravity; thus, virtually no control is given to the operator in increasing or decreasing the percentage of abrasive to air mix used in cutting the glass.

In the pressure-pot system, the hopper is pressurized by the compressor, thus forcing the abrasive into the air line under its own pressure. The result is that much greater control in abrasive to air mix is given to the equipment operator.

Pressure-pot generators can operate over a broader range of pressures, from very low (under 10 psi) to very high (over 150 psi), with extremely precise control in cutting action at every pressure level. Syphon-type generators, on the other hand, must operate in a much narrower pressure range and do not allow the operator to independently control the abrasive to air mix, and thus the cutting action on the glass. In many situations, pressure-pot generators can accomplish the same work as a syphon type in a fraction of the time. For the person interested in cultivating skill in carving or sculpturing, a pressure-pot would almost be essential, particularly if efficiency and consistency are important.

The third type of sand-blast generator, best described simply as a spray gun, is used most often by hobbyists who want to experiment with sand carving prior to purchasing professional equipment, or by anyone whose interest is not related to making professional-quality carvings and sculptures. It is also very attractive to those who wish to make fine airbrush type etchings because the abrasive blast is controlled by a trigger or button mechanism, with very precise on/off control, which is not easily obtained with the pressure-pot.

These miniblasters look just like a spray-paint setup, but instead of putting paint in the canister connected to the spray gun, your abrasive is placed there. The canister will hold a small amount of abrasive, and is suitable for surface etching and light engraving. For the hobbyist who wants to decorate an occasional mirror, glassware, or stained glass project, this should offer an alternative to the two types of units just described. These units work well with small compressors in the 1 to 3 hp range.

Pressure Regulators. This is the piece of equipment that sets the pressure of air delivered from your compressor pressure tank to your sand-blast generator and blasting nozzle. It is most often connected to your sand-blast generator with a short length of pipe. It should have a water and oil filter preceding it in order to prevent these materials from damaging the delicate mechanism used to control air pressure and flow. It is important to note that these gauges will have certain limits of air pressure that can safely be supplied to them; so make sure that the pressure setting on your compressor control switch is not higher than that which can be safely supplied to your pressure gauge. When you are installing this piece of equipment, it is also important to note the direction that the air must flow through the gauge in order for it to operate properly. The direction will be indicated by arrows imprinted on the body of the gauge. If you are working at pressure lower than 100 psi, buy the gauge that is calibrated closest to the range in which you will be working, and that can withstand

the pressure setting on your compressor control switch. Gauges calibrated for operation at higher pressures (150 + psi) are not particularly accurate in the low range (below 30 psi) where most carving and sculpturing is done.

Water and Oil Filters. In association with the air lines connecting your compressor and sand-blast generator, you must have water and oil filters, sometimes called *traps*. They are important for several reasons. First of all, they prevent your abrasive from being contaminated and adversely affecting abrasive flow. Without proper filtration, air lines will, in time, get so much water in them that you will be mud blasting rather than sand blasting. Although this is more critical if you are recycling your abrasive, it is also very important and must be accounted for if you are using silica for blasting and plan only to use it one time. If oil and water are allowed to collect in your air lines, in time they will ruin your pressure regulator and disrupt the abrasive flow.

In selecting water and oil traps, you will find two basic kinds. The first type is sometimes termed a *centrifugal filter*, because its internal construction forces the compressed air to move in circular patterns, with the water and oil molecules being flung to the sides of a chamber, where they collect and fall to the bottom as droplets for removal. Because this action is dependent on the movement of air and is not related to pressure, it is important to make sure your cfm consumption is adequate for the specific filter you will purchase. Generally the larger the filter, the higher the cfm it needs to generate the velocities required to fling the contaminant molecules to the sides of the chamber. Therefore, be sure to match the cfm requirements of your filter to your anticipated consumption.

The second type of filter does not depend on cfm for filtration. It uses a filter material, usually fibrous, through which the compressed air passes. If you are working with relatively low pressures (10 to 30 psi) with a compressor under 5 hp, this will probably be the most efficient filter for you. It is important to remember that the fibrous filters must be changed every so often, depending on how long you blast in a session and the relative humidity in your area. It is best to check these and all filters before and after each blasting session.

Air Lines. Your compressor unit is connected to the sand-blast generator through air lines. These lines can be made from plastic pipe, metal galvanized pipe, or specially constructed rubber hose. Of these, galvanized pipe and rubber hose would be the materials of choice. Metal pipe should be used for all outside installations or where there is any chance of the air line being cut or damaged accidentally. If your air line must be situated near an area where large crates are loaded or unloaded, near the path of fork lifts, or close to large sheets of flat glass, metal is recommended. If you require flexibility in the path of your air line, rubber hose is the only choice. Flexibility of the air line connected directly to the sand-blast generator is recommended, as you will rarely want it to be permanently installed exactly where it is first placed.

When you select air lines, it is important to get a diameter that can deliver the cfm your compressor can produce. The manufacturer's information on a specific compressor unit will suggest the appropriate inside diameter (ID) of air lines necessary to best utilize the capacity of the unit. Some dealers recommend using the largest pipe that will fit into the compressor tank, since it will slow the air flow coming from the tank, and allow the air to cool to a greater degree prior to reaching your pressure regulator and water and oil filters. The cooler the air, the easier it is to filter.

Exhaust Fan. It is most important to account for the removal of dust from a closed room that is having abrasives sprayed into it so that visibility will be maintained and so that the level of dust will be kept at a level that allows respirator masks to work effectively. This procedure is accomplished by use of an exhaust fan, which creates an air flow by blowing out of a vent in the wall of your blasting room. It is important to allow fresh air to enter the room by another vent, thus creating a cross flow of air, which removes the abrasive dust.

Dust Collectors. Now that you are removing this dust-laden air from your blasting room, your local government or neighbors may think you

are polluting the air. The solution is a dust collector (Fig. 2-5). This piece of equipment removes the dust from the air being blown from your blasting room and returns clean air to the environment. Many larger municipal areas require the use of a dust collector in any operation that generates dust. It is not uncommon for exhaust fan/dust collector combinations to be used to efficiently process this dangerous waste material.

Abrasives. The texture of your etched or carved surface will be dependent on the size of grit you use to blast your glass. Most commercial operations use 80- to 120-grit for decorating flat glass. If you think that most of the work you have seen seems a little rough compared to what you would like to obtain, try 140 to 200 grit. If available, purchase or offer to carry away used abrasive from a commercial operation. Dentists or clinics involved in fabricating dentures use very fine grits for removal of casting investments and would be excellent sources for very fine used abrasive. Other sources for coarser used material would be commercial glass decorators or monument makers.

If you are decorating glassware or any other item made from glass that is softer than soda-lime-based float plate glass, 180 to 220 grit and finer will give a very nice, smooth texture, similar to that found on fine copper-wheel engravings.

When you select a particular abrasive, several factors should be considered. First of all, are you planning to reuse or recycle the abrasive? If so, aluminum oxide (the most common for glass decorators) or silicon carbide (the most efficient and most expensive) is recommended. Both of these abrasives can be used a number of times before cutting action is reduced to the point of requiring replacement.

If you are using silica (sand), you cannot indefinitely recycle your abrasive, since it breaks down considerably after use, thus reducing cutting action and the texture imparted to the glass. It also is very easily contaminated with moisture; thus, as it is recycled, its flow characteristics are inhibited. With continued recycling it becomes very inefficient and troublesome.

Blasting Nozzles (Fig. 2-6). The most com-

Fig. 2-5. Ruemelin assembled dust filter with electric bag shaker mechanism and dust discharge valve. This photograph does not show the fan or motor for removing the dust from the blasting room. This is a large commercial unit, generally used by commercial sand carving studios. It allows for the collection of abrasive dusts and recycling of the abrasive. (Courtesy of Ruemelin Manufacturing Company.)

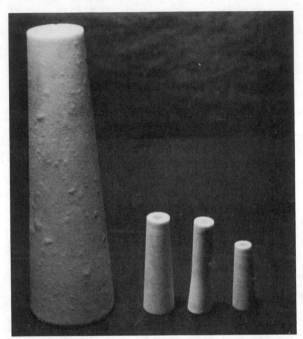

Fig. 2-6. Blasting nozzles. From left to right, #1 blasting nozzle, #2 blasting nozzle, #3L shaping nozzle, #3S shaping nozzle. Smaller nozzles are used for carving and sculpturing smaller designs. The #1 blasting nozzle is the most common for sand carving glass. It is 3 3/4 inches tall. The #3s is 7/8 inch tall.

lection of various orifaces if you use the nozzles for different blasting times. In this way, you don't need to stock various sized nozzles for special applications such as shaded etching or light feathering effects.

If you are doing very small work or are working with a compressor less than 3 hp, you might consider the practicality of using what are termed *shaping* or *carving* nozzles. These are the same shape as the standard #1, but smaller. These nozzles generally come with an oriface of 5/64 or 3/32 inch. They would be useful for decorating glassware, vases, or smaller flat glass items, or sculpturing in an area where very fine control is required. High-relief carving on cameo glass or porcelain is best done with these small nozzles.

mon and popular nozzles are made from high alumina (aluminum oxide) ceramic material that is cast, then high-fired, to vitrification. Other nozzles for commercial production work are made of abrasive-resistant metals. They offer an alternative to anyone working on a large-scale production basis. Whereas a ceramic nozzle will cost slightly over $1, a metal nozzle can cost well over $100.00. Production studies typically find a savings in using the metal types.

Your choices in nozzles will be limited to the overall size of the nozzle and the size of the oriface or hole in the nozzle. The most common nozzle for carving and sculpturing flat glass is the blasting nozzle #1 used by monument markers. This is an excellent nozzle for all types of etching, engraving, carving, and sculpturing. Its size and internal configuration contribute to long wear and good flow characteristics for the air/abrasive mix. By purchasing all of your nozzles with the smallest-sized oriface (usually 1/8 inch), you will soon have a col-

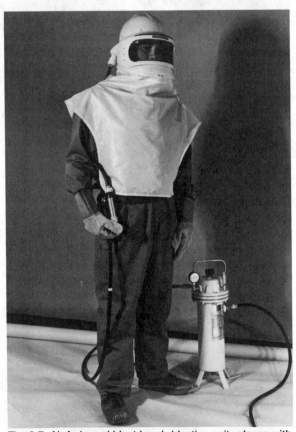

Fig. 2-7. Air-fed sand-blast hood, blasting suit, gloves with air-line filter on floor. Note air-line going into filter, coming from the compressor. Note air flow control unit in operators hand, this controls air flow into the helmet. (Copyright and courtesy of E. D. Bullard Corp., Inc.)

Rough-cutting of your design, or cutting the background away from the design should be done with a #1 nozzle if possible, since it will give you better abrasive flow and a broader cutting area.

Protective Clothing

Protective Head Gear. Because you are working in an environment that is potentially very harmful to your health, it is most important to wear head gear that either furnishes you with fresh air or at least protects you from the reflected abrasive blast, and includes a filter mask (Figs. 2-7 and 2-8). This need cannot be overemphasized.

If you are fortunate enough to have access to an air-fed helmet or suit, it will provide you with the most comfortable and safest method of protecting yourself from the abrasive blasts and resulting harmful dusts. This piece of equipment is supplied air either from your compressor or its own smaller compressor unit (Fig. 2-9) which pumps air directly into it. In either case, it is very important to include a very efficient air filter (Fig. 2-10) between the compressor and the helmet because, with age and use, compressors tend to put oil into the air, and a significant health hazard can result from breathing vaporized oil.

If an air-fed helmet or suit is not available to you, you are safe in using a canvas hood designed

Fig. 2-8. Another shot of air-fed sand-blast hood, blasting suit, and gloves. Operator is in simulated working position. Note the metal nozzle on the end of the blasting hose. This is common in production operations. (Copyright and courtesy of E. D. Bullard Corp., Inc.)

for sand blasting. Because these hoods only serve to protect you from the reflected blast of the abrasive, you must still provide yourself with filtered air to breathe. You can do so easily and safely by using a *respirator mask*, a mask that fits snugly over your nose and mouth and comes with disposable filters designed to remove dusts and particles from the air you are breathing. It is most important to use a mask that is government approved for this purpose and is so designated by being *NIOSH Approved*.

The only type of respirator mask worth trusting your life to is one with flexible rubber construction in the body of the mask, with adjustable head bands and filters that fit into small holders on either side of the mask. These filters should be checked after every blasting session and disposed of when dirty. Such things as "surgeon's masks" or "painter's masks" and most other lightweight masks that do not feature removable filter elements are virtually useless in thoroughly filtering your breathing air. This is one area where no shortcuts should even be considered. Breathing abrasive dusts or silica dusts on a regular basis will result in respiratory problems. The lead time between exposures and subsequent problems can be decades, but the problems will arise given repeated exposures to these dusts and given time to take effect.

The only solution that will prevent you from having problems is to obtain a quality respirator mask, maintain it as directed by the manufacturer, and most importantly make sure it fits properly when it is being used. A poor fit negates the effectiveness of even the best mask.

Clothing. In addition to these special protective devices, you will need clothing to wear while

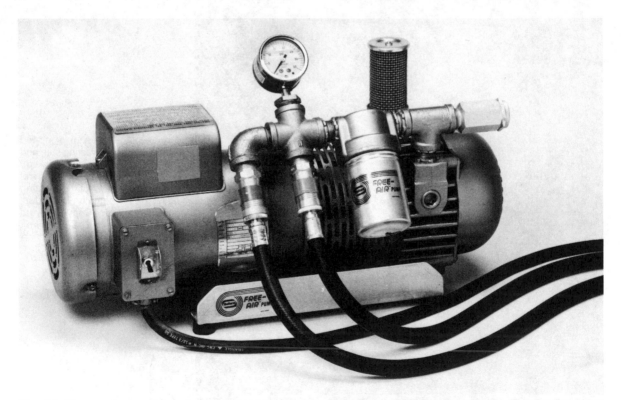

Fig. 2-9. Air pump for supplying air to air-fed hood. Note the air filters before the pressure gauge. This small unit can be used in place of receiving air from a compressor supplying air to a sand-blast generator. This unit is supplying two air-fed hoods, as evidenced by two air hoses coming off the pressure gauge. This unit is useful for the person wanting to add an airfed hood to his set up but who cannot afford a larger compressor needed to supply air to the hood and the sand-blast generator. (Copyright and courtesy of E. D. Bullard Corp. Sausalito, CA 94956.)

you are blasting. A blasting suit, available from the manufacturers of air-fed helmets, is specially designed to maintain the comfort of the operator and not to absorb dusts (Fig. 2-7). If one is not available, you should select some clothing that completely covers your body and will not be used for any other purpose, because most materials become completely saturated with abrasive dusts to the point of almost being uncleanable. Tightly woven, lightweight materials are recommended; cotton knits, denim, corduroy, and flannel are the least appropriate.

Many people find that the reflected abrasive bouncing off the glass hurts their hands. While this problem will depend on the pressure used in blasting and the size of the grit, it is a good idea to wear gloves while you are blasting. Just about any leather- or rubber-coated fabric will do the job.

Assorted Materials

Straightedges. Straightedges are used for measuring your flat glass and placing registration marks on the stencil for positioning the penciled cartoon of the design to be cut. They are also used as guides for making perfect straight cuts with the stencil cutting blade.

Steel Measuring Tapes. Steel measuring tapes are used for measuring your flat glass and openings into which glass must be cut to size.

Large Flat Table. Tables are used to lay the flat glass on while it is being prepared for blasting. It is recommended that these tables be covered with lightweight carpet in order to prevent damage to the glass.

Glass Racks. Glass racks will be required to store the glass during the preparation of the glass for blasting and in the blasting room to hold the glass upright while it is being carved. Simple easels that allow for different height settings of the glass being worked on tend to be best. The fewer the moving parts or metal parts the better, because over time they are destroyed by the abrasive.

For decorative accessories such as vases, bowls, plates, and decanters, a simple shelf should be effective. If you are working with templates, your holders will have to be precisely made to fit the article being decorated since the template must be fit securely and precisely in place. You must generally design your own holders for this purpose, but Patent #3,328,925 illustrates an excellent example which should act as a prototype for anything you would require. You can get a copy of this patent from the United States Patent Office.

Lighting. Because most of the item you are working on is covered with an opaque resist material, your visibility of the item and the design while it is being engraved is at a minimum. This prob-

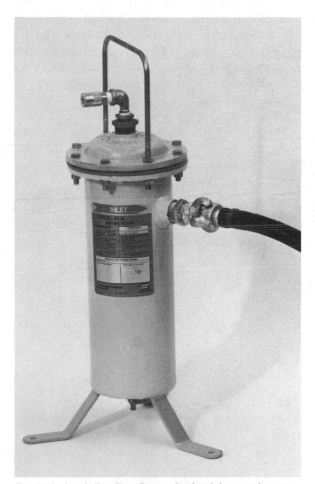

Fig. 2-10. An air-line filter filters air after it leaves the compressor and before it enters the air-fed hood. Note this unit in Fig. 2-7. Note the inlet and outlet (on top of the unit). Air must be run through the filter properly for it to function. It filters moisture, dust and vaporized oil from the air supplied by the compressor. (Copyright and courtesy of E. D. Bullard Corp. of Sausalito, CA 94965.)

lem often necessitates the use of more than one light source to illuminate the area you are blasting. An easy solution is the use of what is commonly known as *utility lights*, which often come with aluminum reflective shields. Two to four of these lights with 150- to 250-watt bulbs should provide enough light for virtually any project. It is important to keep the placement of these lights as flexible as possible because of the different ways you may need to light such items as flashed stained glass, glassware, cameo work, or large panels of flat glass. Because these lights come with rubber-coated clamps, simple wooden racks made from 2 × 4s are inexpensive to make and offer a high degree of flexibility with respect to placement and the angle at which the light strikes the item being decorated.

Opaque Projector. An opaque projector is useful in projecting and enlarging opaque artwork onto paper for pencil tracing and burnishing. In this case, translucent tracing paper is not necessary because the design is projected onto the paper.

Overhead Projector. An overhead projector is useful when artwork is available on a transparent format, such as a film positive.

Pantograph. A pantograph is useful when tracings are to be made of artwork but the degree of enlargement is less than is possible with the two pieces of equipment just mentioned.

Designed Reference Materials. Unless everything you will be doing is totally original and in your own personal style, reference materials form the foundation for renderings of proposed projects.

Project Introduction

3

In this chapter I will familiarize you with the general procedures necessary to make your first projects, and some helpful hints intended to ensure that your first projects come out to your satisfaction. Additionally, I will illustrate a number of different renderings of a few simple designs utilizing Levels 1 to 5 mentioned in Chapter 1. In this way you will be able to graphically see the different tracings that may be necessary for different interpretations of a single design, but more importantly how a single tracing can be the starting point for a number of different renderings showing vastly different skill levels of glass work. Understanding how the original tracing is related to the final appearance on the glass is the first step in learning to interpret all kinds of design sources to a format suitable for your skill level.

The importance of reviewing this section cannot be overemphasized. A few minutes of reading and reflection will allow you to see the designs furnished in Chapter 5 with new eyes. These examples combined with the projects in Chapter 4 offer the first-time sand carving artist the opportunity to con-

sciously choose a level of rendering suitable to his skill level and the application of the finished work. For this reason it is strongly suggested that, if you are making your first project, you thoroughly read Chapters 3 and 4.

Because many of the steps necessary to make high-quality work are very similar, I have put together a list of the basic steps that will apply to virtually any project you will make:

☐ Prepare your glass for application of the stencil material by cleaning with a mixture of 30 percent denatured alcohol and 70 percent water.

☐ Apply and burnish the stencil material onto the glass.

☐ Position your pencil tracing of the engraving design onto the stencil according to your registration marks on the stencil or on your pencil drawing, and tape into place.

☐ Burnish the pencil rendering onto the stencil.

☐ Remove the pencil rendering and cut along the line work that has been transferred to the stencil. Cut the stencil with a cutting blade and handle.

☐ Etch, engrave, carve, or sculpt the design.

☐ Remove all the remaining stencil from the glass after decorating and clean the glass with alcohol and water. Be sure to dry the glass and etched areas evenly to prevent staining.

HELPFUL HINTS

Follow these hints to help make all your designs result in the best possible sand carvings.

Stencil Cutting

Because all of your projects will require the hand cutting of the stencil material, a few points will make this step easier. To begin, you should always start with a new cutting blade to ensure ease of cutting and sharp, smooth lines in your design. If you are a beginner, you will find it easier if you cut by pulling the cutting blade toward yourself, rather than across—from left to right or vice versa—or by pushing the blade while cutting.

The cutting blade should always be kept in a vertical position or leaning slightly forward in the direction of the cut. While cutting you should think of the cutting blade as a sort of "rudder" which must be turned (rotated between the thumb and first three fingers) to make turns and change direction. If you merely pull to the left or right in order to make a turn, you will either pull the blade out of the stencil or risk breaking the blade.

Most importantly, take your time and cut slowly. Stencil cutting is not a race. Pull the blade through the stencil at a rate that is comfortable for your fingers holding the blade handle. If you try to cut too quickly, you will soon develop fatigue in your cutting hand and will tend to waiver from your intended cutting pattern.

Be particularly careful in cutting lettering and graceful curves since slight variations tend to be very evident. When possible, make straight cuts with the aid of a straightedge, keeping the cutting blade turned slightly toward this guide. If you are not careful and do not cut slowly, the blade may come away from this cutting guide, resulting in a poorly cut line.

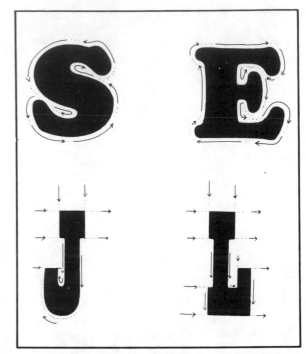

Fig. 3-1. Stencil cutting of letter styles. This illustration shows how the stencil cutting varies with the character of a letter. Full, rounded letters (Souvenir Bold) can be cut in one continuous motion from beginning to end, without ever lifting the cutting blade out of the stencil because there are no sharp corners that must be maintained. The other letter style (Playbill) requires a separate cut for each straight edge because of the sharp corners which must be maintained. Each cut requires that the cutting blade be inserted into the stencil and removed after the cut is made. All cuts must be overlapped slightly in order to ensure easy removal of the stencil after cutting. An overlap of 1/32 inch is adequate. Any design that has interior or exterior corners which must be maintained must be cut in this way.

Tracing Your Intended Design

Your tracing should be made with the softest lead pencil you can find. "Ebony" pencils by Eberhard Faber are particularly good for tracing. With this type of pencil you should be able to obtain multiple burnishings of your design. Tracing should be done on a hard surface with a reasonably (not pinpoint) sharp point.

Sometimes it is recommended that carbon paper be used between your original reference artwork and the rubber stencil in order to transfer the design to the stencil material. You will not find this technique as satisfactory as pencil tracing for a number of reasons. A pencil tracing keeps your reference art in its original condition, rather than being penciled over if carbon paper were used. In using carbon paper, you also run the risk of damaging the reference art through puncturing, because soft rubber stencil is the background on which the tracing is made. Additionally, each repetition of your design requires another tracing, whereas a pencil tracing that is burnished can be used a number of times before retracing is necessary.

In tracing your design, burnishing it onto your stencil, and engraving it, you must be conscious that your design flip-flops a number of times. That is, it is reversed when it is burnished onto the stencil, but then, when your clear glass (intaglio) decoration is completed and turned around for viewing, it is "correct" again.

You must be conscious of different things for each type of engraving.

Reverse Intaglio Engraving. Reverse intaglio refers to clear glass projects in which the design is viewed through the glass after completion. I will refer to the orientation of your original art as "correct." Thus if you have a flower on the right side of your original, and a bird on the left side, that is also the configuration of your pencil tracing. When you burnish it onto the stencil, however, the pattern is reversed, because the pencil side of the tracing paper is applied to the stencil. After burnishing onto the stencil, the flower will be on the left side and the bird on the right side. You then engrave your design in this reversed orientation. Upon completion, however, when you turn your glass around and view the completed decoration through the glass, it is the same as your original.

The same is true of lettering. If you trace the name NANCY, your tracing will read *NANCY*. When you burnish it onto the stencil it will read *YCNAN*, and after you engrave the glass and turn the piece around, it will again read *NANCY*.

The thing to remember is that in a reverse intaglio on clear glass, the glass engraving will have the same left-to-right orientation as your original artwork.

High Relief Engraving. In high-relief engraving, the design is viewed from the same side that it is engraved from—the opposite of a reverse intaglio. Thus, if your flower is on the right side of your original and the bird is on the left of your original, after burnishing onto the stencil this pattern is reversed, again because the penciled side of your tracing was applied to the stencil. After engraving, this reversed orientation remains, because you view the completed decoration from the same side as you burnished it. This is most important to remember if you must have a particular orientation to the completed design, as in the case of lettering. If you trace the name NANCY, when you apply it to your stencil it becomes *YCNAN*, and after engraving it remains *YCNAN*! Therefore, you must either trace high-relief lettering in reverse, or apply dry transfer letters, as I have done in the glassware/decanter projection in Chapter 4.

Again, in high-relief rendering, the finished design maintains the same orientation as the burnished design on your stencil.

Basic Blasting

Because of the different types of equipment that are available, the tremendous range in grit sizes used in sand carving, the different nozzles commonly in use, and the hardness factors of different glasses, it is virtually impossible to give precise directions about how long to blast glass in order to obtain a specific effect. What I can tell you is this: working with a grit from 80 to 120, a pressure setting of 20 to 30 psi, with an 1/8-inch orifice on your nozzle, you will obtain very efficient cutting if you have a visible abrasive flow coming out of your nozzle and can see a flickering ball of light at the point where the blast hits the glass surface. Your nozzle should generally be kept 4 to 8 inches from the surface of the glass. Surface etching, such as refrosting, can be obtained from distances up to several feet, depending on your grit size, pressure setting, and nozzle orifice. If you are interested in working with shaded refrosting, I suggest you cut your pressure down as low as your equipment will allow and begin by working with that setting and the largest orifaced nozzle you have. A large oriface facilitates air flow, and thus abrasive flow, at lower pressures. (See Fig. 3-2.)

If you are working on your first projects, it is important to remember that sand-carved effects are cumulative and are in direct proportion to the exposure of the glass surface to the abrasive blast. What you must do is blast the surface of your design evenly; otherwise you end up with an uneven and unattractive cut. What you should do is determine a pattern of movement of your blasting nozzle over the design and repeat that pattern every 10, 20, or 30 seconds (Figs. 3-3 and 3-4). I suggest you silently count to maintain an even pace throughout the pattern. In time this will become automatic and counting will no longer be necessary. If you are engraving a single motif a number of times (such as corner motifs on flat glass), blast each motif for a number of seconds, then move on to the next, and the next, until you are back where you started. Repeat until the desired depth of cut has been obtained. Do not try to carve each section all at once hoping to match the depth of each

section. You may find this very frustrating, and could cut through the glass trying to get all the depths to match.

During your first projects, it is also very important to remember the relative hardness factors of clear plate glass and stained glass, as opposed to the crystals used in glassware and most decorative accessories. Crystal is significantly softer than flat glass or stained glass, and thus blasts away much quicker. If you have become used to working with plate glass, and try your first full lead crystal glassware, you should reduce your blasting time from 75 percent or more, depending on the thickness of the material and cut your pressure to 15 psi. It is suggested you blast for 5 to 10 seconds then stop and examine the article before you continue. With grits in the 120 to 140 size range, you can easily cut all the way through a common crystal glass in a matter of seconds if you are not careful.

The best procedure for the beginner is to stop blasting and check the depth of cut often until you get a feel for the rate of cutting. This practice will

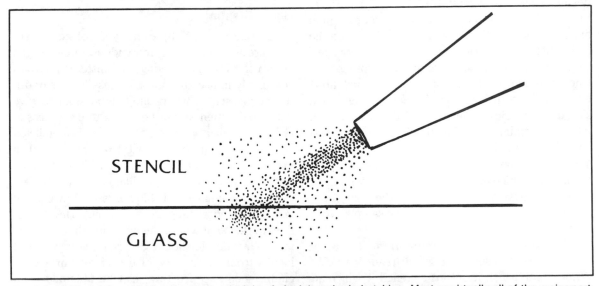

Fig. 3-2. An illustration showing the basic principle of obtaining shaded etching. Most or virtually all of the major part of the abrasive blast is directed at the border between the stencil and the glass. Because a majority of the abrasive is at the center of the blast, with decreasing amounts as you move away from the center, this technique results in a dense etch at the stencil/glass border, with decreasing density of etch as you move away from this border. By varying nozzle distance, orifice size of your nozzle, blasting pressure, grit size, and blasting angle, a very wide variety of effects can be obtained. While this is very simple in principle, and many beautiful designs can easily be executed by the beginner, in practice it can become very complex and difficult within any one design. A major problem is to avoid reetching a previously etched area. Look at the butterfly and rose designs in this chapter for two examples of relatively easy designs for shaded etching.

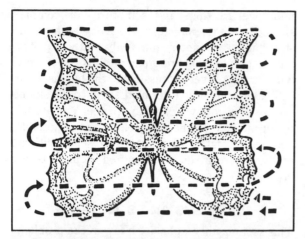

Fig. 3-3. An example of a blasting pattern for the butterfly design shown in this chapter. The arrows indicate the path of the blasting nozzle over the cut stencil design on the glass. The dotted interior of the design represents parts of the glass being blasted. Solid white areas are the stencil material. In this pattern start blasting at the bottom of the design and proceed to the top, then repeat this pattern until the desired depth of cut is obtained.

continue for some time because of the different characteristics of different designs and different types of glasses. This procedure is particularly important if you get into carving or sculpturing.

A SPECIAL NOTE

Obviously, you may not be inclined to spend the money necessary to fully equip a safe and efficient sand carving studio. You are then left with two basic choices: You can either set up an inefficient and unhealthy operation, or more preferably, gain access to someone else's equipment and either do the work of engraving and etching yourself or have them do the work on your already prepared piece of glass.

The ease of finding an accommodating person to help you will probably surprise you. Those businesses that maintain this type of equipment often receive calls from people wishing to utilize its usefulness for a wide range of applications. The most common and accessible facilities that maintain professional sand carving equipment are monument makers and commercial sand-blast companies. Monument makers specialize in engraving and decorating marble and granite for use as

headstones and plaques. Commercial sand-blast companies most often blast the outside walls of buildings prior to repainting or refinishing. They also blast heavy equipment, such as tractor/trailers and land-moving equipment. These firms are easily located by checking in your Yellow Pages under "Monuments" or "Sand-blasting."

If you are in a small-to-moderate-sized community which may not have a professional glass decorating or stained glass studio with the proper facility, you will find these sand-blasting companies and monument makers most accommodating. They often receive requests to blast machine parts, automobile body parts, bicycles, bricks, and virtually anything else that has an outer coating the owner wants removed.

In addition to these companies, you may be able to have your glass engraved by auto body shops, custom motorcycle shops, auto "speed" shops that offer custom machining of parts, commercial or artistic foundries, and dentists or clinics that fabricate dentures. All of these firms will maintain abrasive blasting facilities, although they will be considerable smaller than those at monument makers or commercial sand blasters. In talking to these companies, if they mention they do only *glass beading* and not sand-blasting, they mean they use only fine glass beads as the abrasive. While this is not very useful for efficient deep cutting, it is ex-

Fig. 3-4. Blasting patterns for different monograms and shapes of glassware. Starting at the top or bottom of the design, you should move smoothly and evenly through the entire pattern, and repeat until the desired depth of cut is obtained.

cellent for a very fine surface etch, particularly if you are decorating glassware.

The idea is to allow someone else to do the blasting safely and efficiently, rather than creating the nuisance and hazard associated with abrasive dusts in doing the work yourself in a less than adequate setup.

If you anticipate doing this type of work on a regular basis for profit or anticipate blasting for a few hours at a time on any one project, it is highly recommended that you adhere to all safety precautions with regard to controlling and breathing the resulting dusts. This is particularly recommended for the stained glass artisan who may wish to incorporate sand-carved glass into a small number of projects through the years. The effects of dust inhalation are cumulative; thus, whether numerous exposures are done over a period of years, or condensed into a few days or weeks, it makes no difference; the effects can be disastrous, if not fatal. It may take decades before the effects are recognized, but given adequate exposure to abrasive dusts, you will suffer long-term, permanent damage to your lungs. The cost of a high-quality respirator mask and an exhaust fan is insignificant in relation to the chances you take by not strictly adhering to reasonable precautions.

An alternative that many artisans, craft schools, and hobbyists find useful is the construction or purchase of a well-designed *blasting cabinet*, which is a blasting room in miniature, set up so the operator stands outside and reaches inside through hand holes to manipulate the blasting nozzle and the item being decorated. (See Fig. 2-1.) Often a foot-activated switch is used to supply the compressed air to the nozzle. The paramount concern is to control the dusts resulting from sand blasting so the exposure of the operator to the dusts is minimized. Thus, purchase of a professionally built unit or thoughtful construction of your own unit should make sand carving accessible to virtually anyone with sufficient motivation.

Although it may appear to you, if you are reading these procedures for the first time, that sand carving is a complex and difficult process, that is not necessarily the case at all. Until you get into

multilevel carvings and sculptures or complex shaded etching, all steps are very simple and straightforward, and require only that you pay attention to what you are doing and take your time. Sand carving is very accessible to the beginner, yet is flexible enough to offer challenges to the skilled professional with years of experience. You needn't be intimidated by the complexity that is possible, because no matter what your experience with art or glass, there are literally hundreds of projects that you can do.

PROBLEMS AND SOLUTIONS

This section will emphasize a few of the problems that are common to people working on their first projects. While faithful attention to the previously given instructions would tend to ensure that you avoid these problems, those mentioned tend to be so common, they warrant repeating. The easiest way to avoid problems is simply to pay attention to details and take your time. Some of the health-related precautions have not been mentioned previously, and I suggest that everyone read them.

Glassware

One of the major problems the beginning glass decorator will have with glassware will be cutting too deeply into the glass. The result will be a very fragile item that may break as a result of thermal shock from such innocent sources of temperature change as iced drinks, sunlight, or air conditioning/heater vents. To avoid this problem, keep your pressure low at 10 to 20 psi, your grit fine (180 to 240), and your blasting distance 4 to 8 inches. Check the first item you are blasting after about 10 seconds for depth of cut. The depth is best checked by looking at your engraving in reverse, through the glass. If you have gone beyond the flat etching stage to a point where some degree of form is imparted to the design because of its depth of cut, you have gone about as far as is recommended. With experience, you will be better able to judge the depth of cut on this type of item without removing the stencil material.

If you are decorating a typical wine glass or

other very thin glass, actual engraving is not recommended because the glass walls in this type of item tend to be so thin that they preclude engraving. Thin walls are particularly the case in decorating inexpensive, crystal glass items. If you are decorating a full lead crystal glass with good thickness to the side walls, you could progress to engraving. The key here is to be careful not to cut more than 30 to 50 percent through the material. Only experience and familiarity with your equipment will give you an idea of what you may get away with in executing complex, multilevel engravings on glassware. For the typical monogram or crest design, etching to light engraving is more than adequate for the desired effect.

A second common problem will be *overblast*. While you are engraving the front of your glass, you may be lightly etching the inside surface of the glass with overblast, or that part of the abrasive blast that is not hitting the area at which you are aiming. This is also a problem with stems on wine glasses and the like. The solution is simple. Tape over the top of the glass with masking or duct tape and do the same with the stem or other areas that may be exposed to an indirect blast. Ideally you should mask all areas that might be etched, on purpose or otherwise, especially if someone is doing the etching for you. Make it as easy for them as possible. See Figs. 4-41 and 4-42 for photographs of this additional protection.

A problem during cutting of the stencil by hand also arises at times. Because of the curvature of the glass, it is very easy to get in a position where you are no longer perpendicular to the glass surface with the handle of your cutting blade. The result can be a nonvertical edge on your stencil, leaving a thin edge that may break down during etching or engraving, or an undercut that may not give a perfectly clean edge to your decoration. The only solution is to be mindful of the importance of this vertical position of your stencil cutting knife, and rotate your glass slightly as you are cutting it to maintain this position.

In cutting your stencil, you may notice from time to time a sort of bump bump bump sensation in the cutting action of the blade as it is pulled along the linework of your design. This is not a vertical bump, but one that is horizontal in nature. You're pulling the knife along and you just begin to feel little bumps. What is happening is that the point of your blade has dulled and you are in effect not obtaining a clean, even cut of the stencil. The little bumps indicate small "nibs" or bumps protruding into the design areas you are going to etch. These are usually quite small, but may result in an unattractive edge in some cases. If you are engraving letter styles, these little bumps can destroy the subtlety of a typeface or any other line which must be perfectly engraved in order to obtain the desired effect. The solution is simple—put a new blade into your knife handle. It is also recommended that these nibs be cut from the areas where they have already occurred. While many commercial decorators would say this is not worth paying attention to, it can result in roughly engraved edges if not corrected, particularly if you are working with blasting pressures in the 10 to 20 psi range, using grits of 180 to 240 or finer. Higher pressures with grits in the 80 to 160 range generally blast these features away, thus not requiring correction prior to blasting.

One of the things with which beginning decorators seem to have a lot of problems is proper placement of the design on the glass, whether it is glassware or flat glass, although glassware is more precise due to the smaller size. It is quite disheartening to notice after the work is completed that the design is crooked or placed too high or low on the material. The reason this problem occurs is that you are working on an opaque material in the blasting stencil, which makes it difficult to visualize how the completed transparent piece will look.

The only solution is to be mindful of this potential trouble area, make precise measurements, and double-check them prior to burnishing your design onto the stencil. The placement of precisely measured marks on the stencil once it is on the glass, and corresponding marks on the pencil tracing, which must be matched up prior to burnishing, is one way to avoid this problem. You can also draw precise guidelines into which the design must fit, as I did on the monogrammed glassware in Chapter

4. Flexible rulers or steel tapes are useful for this purpose.

Flat Glass

The problems associated with decorating flat glass, other than the actual carving or sculpturing techniques, are quite straightforward and easily avoided. The solutions take care of themselves through careful execution of the steps in preparing a piece of glass for decorating. You should be mindful, however, that certain things do require attention in order to avoid problems.

First of all it cannot be overemphasized that your glass needs to be cleaned properly prior to application of the stencil. If this is not done, the stencil may lift off the glass during blasting, resulting in a fuzzy edge, or worse, the complete breakdown of a necessary line in your design. As recommended previously, the best thing to use to clean your glass is denatured alcohol and water. A solution of 30 percent alcohol to 70 percent water should clean anything you will find on recently purchased flat glass. You should pay particular attention to the oil residue sometimes left on the edges of the glass after cutting. The cutting wheel is dipped in light oil prior to the cutting of the glass to facilitate the cutting of the glass and lengthen the lift of the cutting wheel.

Another area of potential problems to the beginner is in obtaining an even cut on engraved or carved areas. Because the cutting action of the blasters may be a little hard to see at first, many people do not realize that the cutting of the glass is actually taking place. Consequently they move the blasting nozzle around in a haphazard way, covering the entire design area with an uneven blast. When it appears the design is cut deep enough, they stop blasting and clean the glass, only to discover the design is deeper in some areas than others and the overall appearance is less than expected.

It is important to remember that cutting into the glass with a sand blaster is the result of a cumulative erosion of the surface of the glass. The degree of erosion is directly related to the exposure of the glass to the abrasive blast. Thus, if you blast longer in one area than another, it is cut deeper than surrounding areas. This is logical, straightforward, and easy to understand, but for some reason, many people forget it once they have the nozzle in their hand and are working on a piece of glass.

In order to prevent uneven blasting on your first project, I recommend that you establish a pattern of movement of the blast nozzle that will result in an even blasting of your design (Fig. 3-3). Once this pattern is set up, you should establish a certain speed with which you move through this pattern. Keeping the blast nozzle at a 90-degree angle to the surface of the glass, you should count from 1 to 20, 1 to 50, or whatever every time you make one complete blasting of the entire pattern. Counting will help you maintain the same speed of movement of your nozzle each time you go over your pattern. As you work with carving and sculpturing, this action will become more internalized and second nature to you.

Occasionally, while you are executing a very deep cut piece of work, you may find you have cut all the way through your material. While this possibility is minimized when you are working with 3/8-, 1/2-, or 3/4-inch flat glass, if you have a design with areas wider than the thickness of the glass, it is a possibility. The only solution is to stop during the blasting period and examine the piece of glass from the other side (the side not being blasted). In this way you will get an idea of just how deep you are cutting. In considering deep cutting, you should keep in mind that depth of cut is useful only so far as it adds to the form given to the design. Thus, any depth of cut that does not add to the rendering of your design is superfluous and merely increases your blasting time and reduces the strength of the finished piece. Once you have gotten to the point that your border work or other line work has a fullness in appearance, any additional blasting does not add significantly to the effect of the engraving.

If you notice during blasting that your abrasive flow seems uneven, your sand-blast generator may be low on abrasive. You may also have excessive moisture in your air lines, causing the abrasive to stick together enough to result in an uneven flow into the air line. If you are recycling your abrasive, it may mean that your abrasive has become saturated with moisture and needs to be dried out. Collect all of your abrasive and slowly go over it with a butane or propane torch or put it under a heat lamp for some time to evaporate the moisture trapped in the grit. This condition can progress to the point that abrasive virtually comes out in lumps and sticks to the glass or stencil for a split second before being broken up and blasted off.

It is suggested that your moisture traps be checked at this point (in addition to routine checks) to see if they are full and need to be emptied. You should be particularly aware of this problem if you live in a high-humidity area or must blast while it is raining.

If you are not seeing a round, flickering sphere on the surface of the glass while you are blasting and also do not see the surface of the glass moving during the blasting action, you should increase your abrasive flow. The problem here is that you are probably etching into the glass but cannot determine the rate because it is not visible. Depending on your equipment, you may need to increase the size of your nozzle to facilitate abrasive flow or increase your blasting pressure to facilitate the flow of the abrasive into the line. If you are using a pressure-pot sand-blast generator, a simple adjustment of the abrasive control should suffice and should be tried before you increase pressure or nozzle size. If none of these alternatives changes what you see, you may have too much moisture in your air line, causing the abrasive to stick together and should take the remedies just mentioned.

Health Hints

If you are blasting on a regular basis, you should be aware of the effects of silica dust and abrasive dust on your skin, ears, eyes, and lungs. With simple, easy-to-follow precautions, you should have no health problems resulting from exposure to the microdusts formed during abrasive blasting. Ignoring these precautions can result in serious health problems, particularly with respect to your eyes and lungs.

Over an extended period of time, dust can build up in the pores of your skin and can cause irritation or at least premature aging. Fortunately, this is easily prevented by putting a thin coating of petroleum jelly on your face prior to blasting. After blasting, while taking a shower, simply wash your face to remove this coating and all the dust washes off with the jelly. If you have access to an air-fed hood, you would not experience this problem since no dust comes in contact with this part of your body.

I also recommend that you place cotton balls in your ears in order to prevent excessive buildup of dust and particles in your ears. While this is nothing to be concerned over as far as your general health is concerned, it is a convenient way of keeping difficult-to-clean areas from being overexposed to dust.

Remember that never, under any circumstances, should you rub your eyes while blasting or afterwards, until you have given your eyes a chance to clean themselves or you have flushed them with eye drops. Within a short time after blasting, you should notice a small bit of material in the corner of your eye, at the tear duct. This is the collected dust and debris that got into your eyes while you were blasting. Wearing goggles in addition to a canvas hood and respirator mask (unless of course you have an air-fed hood) will minimize the amount of dust that gets into your eyes, but you will still get small amounts, no matter what you do. After this material has collected at the corner of your eye, it is easily removed with your fingertip. Remember the abrasive cuts glass and the cornea and lens of your eye are much softer and could be damaged if abrasive dust is rubbed into them.

Remember to close your eyes when you are removing your blasting hood after sand blasting because abrasive grit and dust builds up on the hood, and when you remove it, it falls off. If your eyes are open, they will get a good dose of abrasive dust. Closing your eyes precludes this from happening.

When you are putting on your respirator mask, it is most important to make sure you have a proper fit that will prevent any dust from entering the mask. Testing the fit is easily accomplished by placing your hand over the exhalation valve of the mask and exhaling lightly. If you feel resistance to your exhalation, your mask is sealed. Obviously, if you blow hard enough you could succeed in getting the mask to lift off your face, but that is not the object. All you are trying to do is to check and see that you have a good fit.

If any air escapes from around your face, you need to adjust the placement of the mask on your face or perhaps tighten the fit slightly. The area that is generally the hardest to fit is the area under your eyes, on either side of your nose. During the exhalation test, you may notice a cool sensation under your eyes. This indicates air flow out of the mask into your eyes, and should be corrected prior to blasting.

There are a number of flexible respirator masks on the market, each of which will have a slightly different configuration designed to fit your face. Not all masks fit all faces. If you find the mask you have purchased simply will not adjust to your face, you should take it back to your dealer. If the mask is unused, you should have no problem exchanging it. If you have used it, even once, this may not be the case. In trying to make a mask fit, you should not have to resort to adjusting the head bands so tight that headaches or pinching of your skin results. A good mask is designed to be worn for many trouble-free, comfortable hours.

If during blasting you suspect that abrasive is getting into your mask and into your mouth, you should stop blasting and check immediately. An easy test is to very lightly grind your teeth together. If you feel grit between your teeth, you should cut off your sand-blast generator and leave the blast room immediately. Once outside, remove your mask, and look inside. If you have had a leak, you should see dust inside your mask. The mask must then be washed and cleaned to remove this dust before you put it back on and continue blasting.

If you are fortunate enough to have access to an air-fed hood that supplies fresh, filtered air, you need to be mindful of the filtration system. If it is the kind that needs to be emptied, check it before each blasting session. If it uses removable or replacable materials in filtering, these materials should be carefully maintained. The reason is sim-

ple. Because this air is supplied by a compressor, it may tend to have water vapor or oil vapor suspended in it. The oil content will tend to increase with the age of the compressor, while the water content is related to the humidity and the efficiency of your water traps. Needless to say, breathing oil vapor for any period of time could be injurious to your health. If you have access to someone else's equipment, you should make sure it is properly maintained prior to using it.

COMPARATIVE DESIGNS

The photographs in this section show some simple designs that have been etched, engraved, carved, and sculptured in different ways so that you see the work and skill level involved in each type of rendering. For the hobbyist or beginning glass artist, this is one of the most important sections in this book with respect to illustrating how you progress from a sketch or idea to a specific glass rendering. By reading the descriptions of these renderings and looking closely at each design, you will see the number of alternatives that must be considered when you are rendering even very simple designs. This added insight into sand carving techniques should help hobbyists and beginning glass artists progress relatively quickly to more advanced levels of work. It will also help professional buyers of sand-carved glass communicate with their glass designers. Even if you feel that you cannot design an original glass carving because of a lack of formal training or natural ability in art or drawing, this section should help you see how to interpret reference art into a format that you can make for yourself.

If you recall, in Chapter 1 I made up a sequence of levels of sand-carved renderings, relating to skill level and degree of difficulty in designing, conceiving, and executing the work.

This sequence was:

1) Single-level etching
2) Single-level engraving
   a) Single-level deep-cut
3) Engraved line work with
   a) solid etching

b) shaded etching
4) Carving
5) Sculpturing

Generally speaking, the level of difficulty increases as the numbers increase. Levels 1 through 3a are very accessible to the first time sand carver and are very useful for many commercial applications. If you are just beginning to experiment with sand carving or are working on your first projects, this is very important to remember. In many cases you will find that if a particular design takes 1 hour of work to produce a single-level deep-cut engraving, 1 hour and 10 minutes (or less) may give you a Level 3a rendering, with the added attractiveness and sophistication of a multilevel rendering. The additional time required to produce the more advanced work is insignificant in relation to the basic time and effort necessary to produce the simpler rendering. Therefore, a little extra effort can result in a markedly more attractive finished design.

Once you have progressed to shaded etching (Level 3b), carving (Level 4), and sculpturing (Level 5), the skill level increases many times over the simpler renderings. It is important to remember, however, that with a little practice, a very useful level of skill can be developed with these techniques. After you understand the basic concepts involved in designing for this type of work, you will probably surprise yourself with the quality of work you can produce. These techniques also offer a degree of complexity and versatility that will challenge even the most adept designer/glass artist for years. For those interested in advanced techniques, particularly carving and sculpturing, I have included projects and more detailed descriptions of how to design for them in Chapter 7.

Progressing to sculpturing (Level 5) is a quantum leap forward in technical difficulty with respect to conceiving and executing the rendering. Because sculpturing indicates the controlled shaping of the glass surface within each section of the design (as opposed to layering indicative of carving alone) into a modeled bas-relief which can obtain a very high degree of subtle form—it is a technique that usually requires some years of practice before a thorough

degree of understanding of the potential and difficulties can be grasped. This is not to say the talented novice will not be able to produce many beautiful sculptured designs within a relatively short period of time. I am simply saying that anyone experimenting with sculpturing should understand they will be learning for many years.

In examining the following examples, you will see why it is very difficult to decide on precise definitions of such descriptions as engraved, carved, deep-cut, and sculptured. You will see why my sequence of levels is somewhat arbitrary, and is useful more for introductory explanations of this type of work, rather than for a scale or classifications system for the various renderings that are possible through sand carving, particularly when multiple effects have been incorporated into a single design motif. Hopefully, the labels I have applied to these renderings will give way to your being able to see the work, and not merely apply limiting definitions to the techniques used.

Materials Used

All of the following examples were executed on 1/4-inch-thick clear float plate glass, using 220-grit silicon carbide. For blasting I used a 5 hp, 17 cfm compressor and a Ruemelin pressure-pot sand-blast generator with a #1 blasting nozzle, 1/8-inch orifice. All designs were hand-cut using a #11 X-Acto blade, with "Buttercut" stencil being used as the sand-blast resist (Figs. 3-20 through 3-25). The blasting pressure ranged from 12 to 30 lbs., with deep-cutting and solid etching done at the higher pressures and shaded etching, carving, and sculpturing done at the lower pressures.

All of the designs are between 2 and 6 inches across and could be executed with a compressor in the 1 to 2 hp size range, using virtually any type of sand-blast generator described in Chapter 2. Thus, these renderings illustrate the type of work that is possible with less-than-professional-level production equipment. You don't need sophisticated equipment to experiment and learn sand carving, but it is definitely worth the expense if you are going to be doing this type of work on a professional or continuing basis.

Butterfly

The butterfly is shown in Figs. 3-5 through 3-9. Its size is 5 × 5 inches.

Figure 3-5. This rendering could be described as a single-level engraving (Level 2) or a single-level deep-cut engraving (Level 2a). It is deep cut because the depth of cut results in a fullness to the line work that is consistent with its width. The depth of cut results in a more glowing appearance than if it were merely surface etched. If any more blasting were done, some areas would be peaked out, which would take more time, but would not enhance the sculptural appearance of this design.

All of the line work in Fig. 3-20 was traced and burnished onto the stencil, then hand-cut. Note that I have labeled two areas in this tracing—Section 1 and Section 2. Section 1 corresponds to all of the areas cut into the glass; thus, that part of the stencil was removed, exposing those areas to the abrasive blast. All of the areas in Section 2 were left with the stencil on the glass during the blasting step, thus they remained clear. This type of rendering is one of the easiest to make, and is particularly good if you are having someone do the blasting for you.

Figure 3-6. This rendering is an example of engraved line work with solid refrosting (Level 3a). It is virtually identical to Fig. 3-5, except that after the line work (Section 1) was deep-cut, I removed all of the stencil from all parts of Section 2 and surface-etched those parts. This can generally be accomplished with a single pass of the blasting nozzle. Compare this photograph with the appearance of Fig. 3-5. The difference in difficulty and time in production is minimal between these two renderings, yet Fig. 3-6 offers a more sophisticated multilevel appearance.

This is an excellent way for hobbyists to obtain multilevel effects in their first projects. If you are having someone do the blasting for you, you could easily do this type of rendering if you are present to remove the stencil from those areas that are to be etched after the deep cutting of the line work. This is particularly true if you have a number of sections that must be removed for the refrosting step, since some businesses that will blast your work may not be inclined to hand-pick your stencil for you. By calling ahead and making arrangements to have the work done while you wait, you should be able to obtain this type of rendering with someone else doing all of the blasting.

This type of rendering is excellent for the person who wants to decorate a rather large area and wishes to minimize the blasting time. Simply outline your design as I have done, deep-cut all of the linework, and refrost all of the interior areas. Refer to Project #3 for another example of this type of rendering.

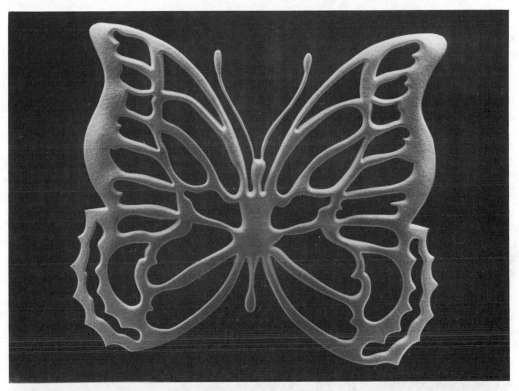

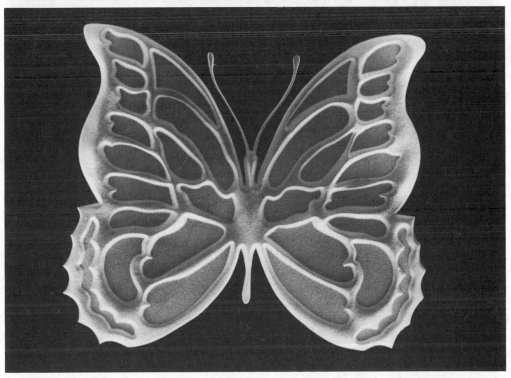

Figure 3-7. Like the two previous renderings, this one is based on the line drawing of Fig. 3-20. In this example, however, I reversed the order of steps used in making Fig. 3-6. For this bulbous, and relatively unattractive rendering, I first deep-cut all sections labeled Section 2, then removed the stencil from Section 1, which was then surface etched.

This is an example of a rendering that is sculpturally inappropriate. The result is a flat-bodied butterfly, with bulbous areas projecting from the wings. Technically, this is a well executed rendering, in that all of the deep cutting is even and full, and all stencil cutting is smooth and clean. Yet, the result is less than pleasing to the eye.

Figure 3-8. This rendering is more sophisticated than the previous three examples of the butterfly design. For this example, I based my glass design on the line drawing in Fig. 3-21. For those who want to see how different tracings affect the final appearance on the glass, it is very important to compare Fig. 3-20 with Fig. 3-21. Note that the "body" of the butterfly is delineated in Fig. 3-21 rather than being continuous with the wings, as in Fig. 3-20. This is a very important difference, which you can easily note by comparing Fig. 3-6 with Fig. 3-8. It is also very important to note the difference between those parts I referred to as Section 2 in Fig. 3-20 and the comparable parts of Fig. 3-21. In Fig. 3-21 these sections have been expanded until they directly share borders, rather than have spaces between them, as in Fig. 3-20. You will also note that these sections have been sequentially numbered from 3 through 16. These numbers correspond to the sequence which must be followed in obtaining the results shown in Fig. 3-8.

If we were to classify this rendering according to the levels previously mentioned, this could be classified an example of carving (Level 4) and shaded etching (Level 3b). It is a carving because Sections 1 and 2 (Fig. 3-21) were engraved sequentially, resulting in the separation of the body (Section 1) from the outline of the wings (Section 2). After this was accomplished, each section from 3 to 16 in the wing was sequentially exposed to the edge of the abrasive blast, resulting in the shaded etching. (See Fig. 3-4.) In this design matching sections of the wings on both sides were etched at the same time; i.e., when Section 3 on the left side was etched, the matching section on the right side was also etched. By doing both sides simultaneously, the risk of accidentally reetching any of the already etched sections was minimized. Reetching exposed sections of your design will be a major problem in executing shaded etchings. Careful planning, low blasting pressures, and experience are virtually the only ways to avoid ruining this type of work. In working with shaded etching, it is very important to remember that you have only one pass of the blasting nozzle in order to obtain the desired effect. With a little practice, you will probably surprise yourself with the subtle shaded effects you can obtain. If you work with this particular technique, you will also soon appreciate how complex and difficult it can become on apparently simple designs. Compare Fig. 3-15 with Figs. 3-16, 3-18 and 3-19.

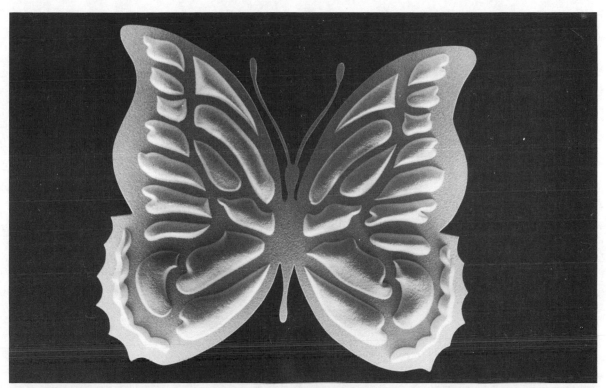

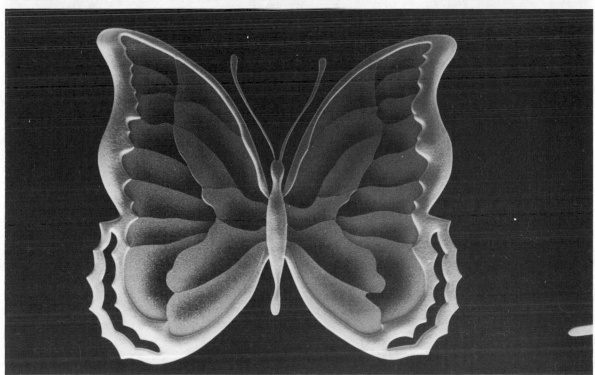

Figure 3-9. For this rendering, the line-drawing (Fig. 3-21) was used as in the previous example. I did vary the sequence of a few steps, and sequentially carved sections 3 through 16 rather than refrosting them. The result is a dramatically different appearance. The time involved in producing this rendering was also significantly greater than that necessary for the previous rendering. Is the extra time and effort worthwhile? In many applications, particularly in rendering a subject that is to suggest lightness or delicacy, the weighty appearance of this rendering is not worth the effort. This is an excellent example of the importance of matching the character of the subject with the style or technique of rendering.

This rendering was done in this order, referring to Fig. 3-21; Section 1; Section 17 (very deep cut); Sections 3 through 16, carving both sides simultaneously; then Section 2, with solid etching top and bottom and shaded etching on the sides of the wings.

Fleur-de-Lis

The fleur-de-lis is shown in Figs. 3-10 through 3-13. Its size is 3 1/2 × 3 1/4 inches.

Figure 3-10. In this series of renderings I have used a copyright-free design from a source given in Chapter 6 as the basis for the glass design (see Fig. 3-22). I traced Fig. 3-22 in order to adapt it to the glass work. For this rendering, I first deep-cut Section 1, then deep-cut Section 2. Note the relative lack of fullness to Section 2, immediately adjacent to the previously cut Section 1. If I had blasted this area in the same way as the rest of Section 2, it would have distorted the previously cut section. In order to prevent this from happening, I backed off slightly to maintain the integrity of Section 1. This is a very important principle to remember when you are working on your own carvings (Level 4). After these sections were deep-cut, I removed the stencil from Sections 3, 4, and 5 above and below the cross bar (Section 1) and simply surface-etched them.

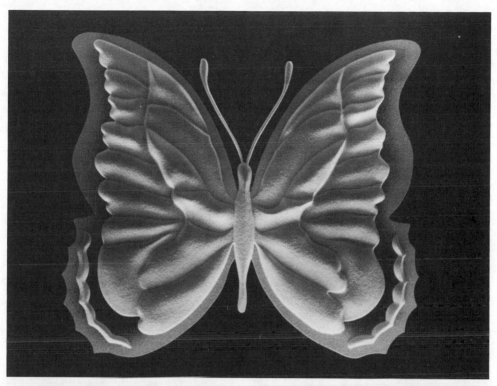

Figure 3-11. In this rendering I have combined deep-cutting, solid refrosting, and shaded refrosting. First Section 2 was evenly deep-cut all the way around the entire design. Compare the parts of Section 2 immediately adjacent to Section 1 in this rendering with that of Fig. 3-10. This will help you see the relatively flat parts of Section 2 in Fig. 3-10 mentioned in the description of that rendering. After deep-cutting Section 2, the stencil from Section 1 was removed and given a solid refrost. A single pass of the blasting nozzle was all that was necessary for this step. Next the stencil from Section 3 was removed with shaded etching being added on both sides of that section. A single pass down each side of this section was all that was necessary. Next the stencil from Section 4 was removed, with shaded etching being added only on the top edge. This was repeated for Section 5, thus completing the design. This rendering is far more suggestive of form than that in Fig. 3-10 when viewed from a distance of a few feet, although it is not apparent in this close-up photograph.

Figure 3-12. This rendering combines controlled deep cutting and solid etching. It took considerably more time and skill than Fig. 3-11; yet from a distance of only a few feet, it is no more suggestive of sculptural form. This is an excellent example of where the actual form of the glass is not as suggestive of *sculptural fullness* as the suggested form obtained with shaded refrosting in the previous example (Fig. 3-11). It illustrates the illusory quality of sand-carved glass that will confound beginning glass designers. Only experience will tell you when to use this characteristic of glass to advantage.

For this rendering, I first deep-cut Section 1, then Sections 3, 4, and 5 were deep-cut in that order. Note that each of Sections 3, 4, and 5 was cut with increasing fullness from the edge to the center. Each of these areas was deliberately shaped, and not mechanically blasted, in order to obtain a full deep cut. Notice the tapering depth of cut as these sections pass "under" Section 1, which is, again, indicative of purposeful shaping and not mechanical blasting. After these sections were deep-cut, Section 2 was given a solid etching, establishing the border of the entire motif. In considering the time and skill necessary to execute this rendering, and the fact that it is not as suggestive of sculptural form as the rendering in Fig. 3-11, for most applications it would not be the rendering of choice.

Figure 3-13. This rendering was executed exactly like that in Fig. 3-10, except that after refrosting Sections 3, 4, and 5, these sections were carefully shaped to suggested fullness. The depth of cut here is substantially less than in Fig. 3-12, but the suggestion of form is substantially greater, because of the relative depth of cut of all of the sections of the motif. The different depths of cut work together in suggesting form, rather than depending on actual depth of cut to suggest this characteristic. This is another example of the illusory character of sand-carved glass.

For the beginning glass artist, it may yield surprising results if in addition to simply refrosting those areas within deep-cut line work, you try to carefully add some degree of fullness. The results will surprise you.

Rooster

The rooster is shown in Figs. 3-14 through 3-16. Its size is 4 1/4 × 5 inches.

Figure 3-14. This rendering is based on the line drawing Fig. 3-24, and is used as the design for Project #3 in Chapter 4 illustrating engraved line work and solid refrosting. (The numbering on Fig. 3-24 is used for rendering Fig. 3-15.) In this rendering, I traced the design exactly as it is shown in Fig. 3-24; however, when cutting the stencil I cut on both sides of the pencil lines, allowing me to remove all of the stencil from the within design while leaving the stencil corresponding to the pencil lines in the tracing. In this way the interior areas of the design is etched or engraved, and the tracing lines are left clear. Figure 3-14 is cut into the glass enough to catch the light to some degree, but is not cut to a depth to give any sculptural form to the design. Thus, this rendering could be classified as single-level engraved (Level 2) or single-level deep-cut (Level 2a).

This is one of the easiest types of renderings to make, since all the areas to be cut into the glass are blasted at one time. No multiple steps are required, and only even blasting is necessary to obtain the effects shown in this rendering. If you are having someone else blast your work for you, this type of rendering would be particularly easy for them to do. Although it is very difficult to obtain any sculptural effects with this type of rendering, it is easy for the first-time sand carver to do and is very popular for commercial installations due to its low cost. Look at Figs. 3-6 and 3-10 and Project #3 in Chapter 4 for alternatives to this very basic type of rendering, which are also accessible to the first-time sand carver, and very appropriate for commercial installations.

Figure 3-15. In this rendering Fig. 3-24 was also used as the basis for the glass design. However, I have deeply sculptured each section numbered 1 through 26. The numbers in Fig. 3-24 correspond to the sequence in which each section was cut into the glass. This rendering could accurately be described as sculptured. Virtually every area has been purposefully shaped to correspond to its function within the design, and to represent the form of each anatomical part of the original image, that of a chicken. Obviously this is a very stylized version of the subject, but I have tried to be conscious of the form of each separate part of the image. Note the tapering fullness of the two combs, the fullness and form given to the chest and forewing areas, and the angularity given to the wing feathers. Each of these forms was preconceived and purposefully cut into the glass. Although this type of rendering is generally beyond the ability of the beginning glass carver, by following the sequence I have furnished in Fig. 3-24, you will probably surprise yourself with the multilevel appearance of your first piece following this blasting sequence. If you are interested in this level of work, I suggest you read the Advanced Projects in Chapter 7.

Figure 3-16. In this rendering Fig. 3-24 was used again, as it was in rendering Figs. 3-14 and 3-15. However, by altering the sequence of steps and techniques used in the rendering, I obtained a markedly different appearance to the glass design. This rendering combines sculpturing (Level 5) and shaded etching to advantage. Although this rendering may be too advanced for beginning sand carvers, it is interesting to see how altering the sequence of steps in making the design alters the final appearance on the glass. This rendering should also be of interest to buyers of sand-carved glass as an example of a combination of relatively advanced techniques, using each to obtain a measure of sculptural form.

The sequence followed in obtaining this rendering was: first to deeply cut and shape Sections 1, 2, 3, 5, 6 and 14. After the deep cutting, the shaded etching was added as follows: Sections 4, 7, and 9 through 13, then 15 through 26. By comparing this sequence with that used in Fig. 3-15, you can see that the basic sequence was followed in both renderings, particularly when you come to the obviously sequential design elements such as the wing and tail. The difference between these two renderings was that all of the deep cutting was done first, then shaded etching added in Fig. 3-16; whereas in Fig. 3-15, each section was deeply cut and shaped.

Rose

The rose is shown in Figs. 3-17 through 3-19. Its size is approximately 2 × 2 inches.

Figure 3-17. In this rendering of a rose, the same technique was used as in the first Rooster rendering (Fig. 3-14). The line drawing used for this rendering was Fig. 3-25. As in Fig. 3-14, all of the lines in the original line drawing were traced and burnished onto the stencil, which was then cut on both sides of the pencil lines with all sections of stencil removed at one time, and all blasting accomplished in one step. Like the Rooster in Fig. 3-14, the results of this technique is that the different sections of the design appear to be unconnected and seemingly to float apart from each other. Regardless of the depth of cut, little sculptural form can be accomplished with this type of rendering. This rendering was cut relatively deep, and could thus be described as a single-level engraving or single-level deep-cut (Level 2 or 2a) rendering.

For hobbyists and beginning glass artists, a more pleasing rendering of this design could be made by engraving the line work between the presently engraved segments and refrosting the sections that have been engraved. See Figs. 3-6 and 3-10 and Project #3 in Chapter 4 for this type of rendering.

Figure 3-18. Except for the engraved stems (note the depth of cut on the leaf stems), this rendering is made up exclusively of shaded etching. The light and shadow effects of this type of etching result in the suggestion of form in this rendering, rather than the suggestion of form coming from depth of cut.

Again Fig. 3-25 was used as the basis for this rendering. The sequence in obtaining these effects is slightly different than the numbering on Fig. 3-25 which was used for the Level 5 rendering of the Rose in Fig. 3-19. I engraved and etched this rose in this sequence: Sections 16, 1, through 14, then 17 through 25, and 26 through 34. Note that Section 15 was left clear (unetched); thus, the stencil was left on this area throughout the making of this rendering. Because this design is so small (just under 2 inches in diameter), these very small sections would be impossible to obtain a suitable shaded etching effect. Thus they are left clear, which in reality lets them drop away into the background when viewed in natural light. The high contrast of this photograph makes them stand out more than when viewed in person.

If you wish to experiment with shaded etching, this is an excellent design to work with. The sequence of steps is furnished for you, and you have an example to use as a reference. Learning to control the precise etching of such small areas is excellent practice, since it will give you experience in learning about the intricacies involved in relatively simple designs such as this one. Your biggest problem will be to avoid reetching already etched sections of the design. Only experience and planning will help you avoid this problem.

61

Figure 3-19. This rendering is the most sculpturally complex example of Level 5 work contained in this chapter. Like the two previous rose designs, it is based on Fig. 3-25. The numbering on this line drawing corresponds exactly to the sequence of steps used in making this rendering. Note the difference in form given to the glass between comparable sections in Figs. 3-17 and Fig. 3-19. The line drawing is identical; only the manipulation of the blasting nozzle and sequential removal of the stencil makes these two renderings so different. This rendering is also far more sophisticated than the sculptural work in Fig. 3-15. In Fig. 3-15, I cut some degree of fullness or angularity in the glass; however, in this rose motif, a wide variety of shapes and effects are contained in the petals of the flower. Look at the full round areas within the petals, and the ridges and points that rise and fall around the edges of the petals. Each of these characteristics was preconceived and purposefully executed to obtain this rendering. Considering that this type of work is sculptured in reverse with minimal visibility during the blasting, you can begin to understand why a good deal of practice may be necessary before you will be able to obtain these effects in your work. While you may not be able to initially make this type of rendering for yourself, it is important to see how even relatively simple designs can become the basis for sculpturally complex renderings. The same line drawing was used for Figs. 3-17 through 3-19, yet look at the different effects and appearance that is possible based on stencil and nozzle manipulation. This difference graphically illustrates the fact that the final glass rendering is based more on your skill and insight into sand carving than any limitation inherent in a line drawing.

In looking at this rendering, take note of the obtrusive angularity of the leaves. This type of look is sometimes characteristic of what is called *carved glass*. It lacks subtlety in relation to the rest of the rendering and communicates nothing of the form or character of the leaves of a plant. It is neither skillfully stylized nor realistic. The stems lack continuity with the leaves, so the leaves look like they are about to fall off. The stylistic and technical difference between the rendering of the flower itself and the leaves destroys any unity between these design elements. This points up the importance of stylistic continuity between the different elements of any glass design, particularly more sophisticated renderings.

For buyers and designers of sand-carved glass, this point is very important to remember. The technique and quality of rendering of design elements within any composition must complement each other. Otherwise a lack of unity results, with disastrous results in the overall appearance of the finished work.

For beginning glass artists and others interested in more advanced techniques in sand carving, this rose serves as an example for reference and practice. You have been given the exact line drawing and sculpturing sequence necessary to obtain the effects you see. You should also remember that this rose is slightly less than 2 inches across at the widest point; thus, large compressors and sophisticated pressure-pot sand-blast generators are not necessary to begin to experiment with sophisticated glass sculpturing techniques.

63

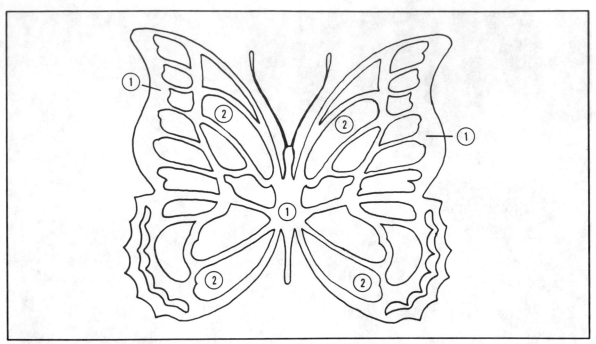

Fig. 3-20. Line drawing used for glass renderings shown in Figs. 3-5 through 3-7.

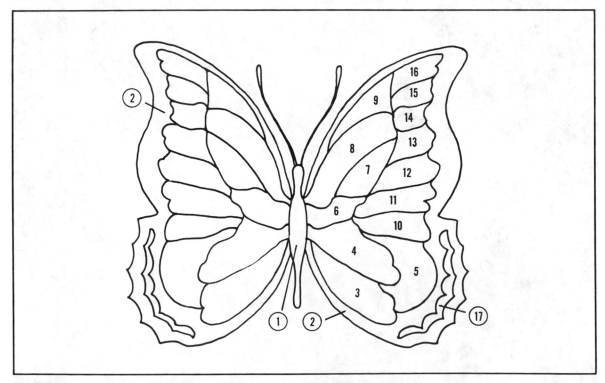

Fig. 3-21. Line drawing used for glass renderings shown in Figs. 3-8 and 3-9.

Fig. 3-22. Original camera-ready art used for glass renderings in Figs. 3-10 through 3-13.

Fig. 3-23. Tracing of Fig. 3-2 used for glass renderings in Figs. 3-10 through 3-13.

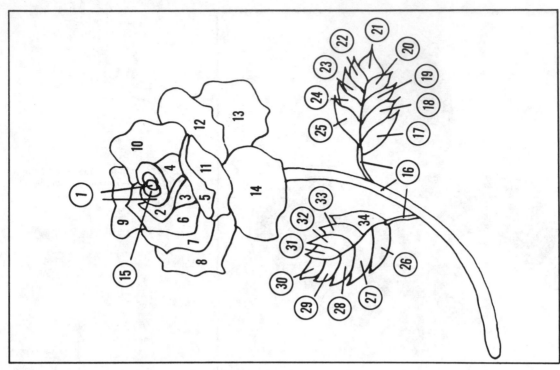

Fig. 3-25. Line drawing used for glass renderings in Figs. 3-17 through 3-19.

Fig. 3-24. Line drawing used for glass renderings in Figs. 3-14 through 3-16.

Beginning Projects

The beginning level projects in this chapter are intended to act more as examples of the basic steps necessary to execute intaglio and high-relief sandcarved designs on a variety of materials and objects, than as projects to faithfully copy. These are beginning points for your own work and not dead-end projects that teach you nothing about the principles necessary to design and engrave your own original projects. Each project illustrates far more than how to decorate the particular type of item shown or the design illustrated. I suggest that you read and review every project before you make your first project so you will be aware of alternative techniques that may not be contained in one project but that are shown in another. For example, while you may have no interest in engraving a glass plate, you may find the type of rendering in that project is very useful for your flat glass work. Each project in this chapter is designed with the beginner in mind, and all techniques and processes shown are accessible to the first-time sand carver.

The following description of each project will give you an idea of how the techniques shown may be applied to other projects and how other materials may be substituted.

Border Motif on Flat Glass. This project shows a border design that is deep cut and etched on clear float plate glass. It should act as an example for all of your flat glass projects on plate glass, mirrors, or flashed stained glass. Border designs are some of the most popular because of their applications on windows, mirrors, picture frame glass, doorways, etc. I have included many border designs in the next chapter for your projects.

Glassware and Decanter Monogramming. This project shows intaglio and high-relief engraving of lettering on curved and flat surfaces. Because of the very wide applications of engraved lettering, this is a very important project. Also shown is a decanter that was purchased at an estate sale for a fraction of its current replacement retail value, illustrating an important source for high-quality engraving blanks for the nonprofessional.

Multilevel Engraved and Etched Plate. This project illustrates the easiest and most accessible method of obtaining multilevel effects in your engravings. This type of engraving and etching combination is applicable to virtually any flat glass or decorative accessory-type item. It is efficiently and easily executed by the novice, yet results in a very sophisticated look on the glass. If you are decorating relatively large pieces of glass (over 24 inches in any dimension) and have access only to a small compressor (2 hp or less), this is a very efficient way of decorating large areas without lengthy blasting. This project shows you how to engrave only the outlines of your design, then fill in the majority of the area of the design with etching. The plate that is engraved was purchased at a flea market for a fraction of its retail value, illustrating another source of quality engraving blanks for the nonprofessional.

Intaglio and High-Relief Combination Engraved on a Ceramic Plate. This project is significant in that it illustrates an opaque material being sand-carved, thus acting as an example for work on ceramics, porcelain, stone (brick, marble, granite, slate), or opaque glass. Ceramic and porcelain blanks are available as plates, tiles, bells, and a number of other items from arts and crafts suppliers dealing with "China Painting," thus, the techniques shown apply to many more items than that illustrated. Additionally, tips are given which should mean that your first high-relief projects in opaque materials will come out to your satisfaction.

BORDER MOTIF ON FLAT GLASS

This first project will introduce all of the basic procedures and materials necessary to sand-carve virtually any flat glass project, whether plate glass 1/4 through 3/4 inch thick or mirror. This project shows a design being rendered in Levels 1 and 2a; that is, etching part of the design and deep-cutting (single-level) another part of the design. See Figs. 4-1 through 4-16. These two levels of sand-carved decorations are by far the most popular and accessible to the beginning glass artist or hobbyist. Using this type of rendering and referring to the design section of this book, or the additional sources of designs listed in Chapter 6, you should be able to generate literally hundreds of projects for yourself.

The design illustrated in this project is very

Fig. 4-1. Peeling the white vinyl sheet away from the adhesive side of the stencil material. The darker layer on the bottom is the actual rubber stencil sheet.

Fig. 4-2. With the stencil on the bottom, peel back a few inches of the vinyl cover sheet. Turning the stencil material under, apply it to the edge of the glass to be decorated.

Fig. 4-3. Reach under the stencil material, moving your finger forward slowly, and apply the stencil a few inches at a time. Peel back the vinyl layer as necessary.

Fig. 4-4. The stencil has been flipped forward to show the position of the hands under the stencil while it is being applied to the glass. The area of the glass in front of the hands does not have the stencil applied to it yet.

Fig. 4-5. An alternative to the fingertip method of stencil application. Once the stencil is begun (1 to 2 inches on the glass), use one hand to hold the stencil up and forward (left hand in the picture). Using a glass (or roller brayer) in the other hand, roll the glass forward and backward in short movements to apply the stencil to the glass.

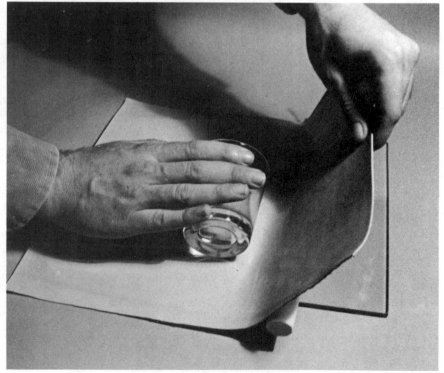

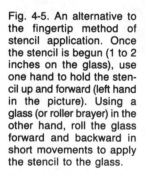

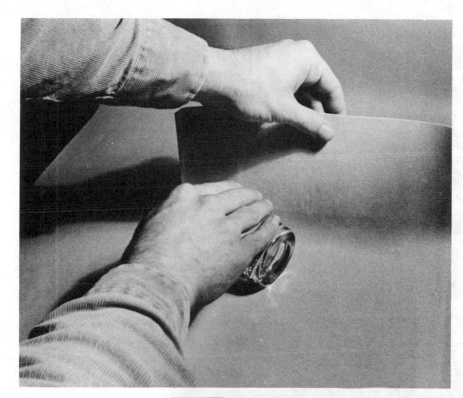

Fig. 4-6. Another view of Fig. 4-5.

Fig. 4-7. Once the entire stencil is applied to the glass, place a piece of wax paper on the stencil and using the bottom of a glass, rub the stencil firmly into place.

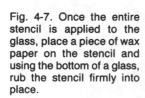

Fig. 4-8. Turn the flat glass over and trim excess stencil from the edges.

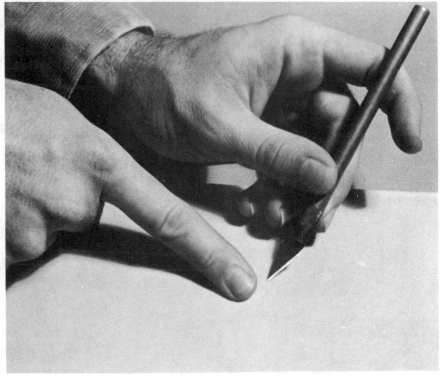

Fig. 4-9. After burnishing with the wax paper, you will notice bubbles of air between the stencil and the glass. These will be very obvious by looking at the stencil surface. Only those bubbles that overlap with your design must be removed. Using the point of your cutting blade, puncture one side of the bubble, and simultaneously press on the other side of the bubble with your finger. The pressure from your finger will force the air out of the bubble through the small hole you cut with your cutting blade.

72

Fig. 4-10. Using registration marks, the design is positioned onto the stencil and burnished using the bottom of a glass. The registration marks are on the pencil tracing and match the corner of the glass. Burnishing is accomplished by pressing firmly as the glass is moved in small circular motions over the pencil tracing.

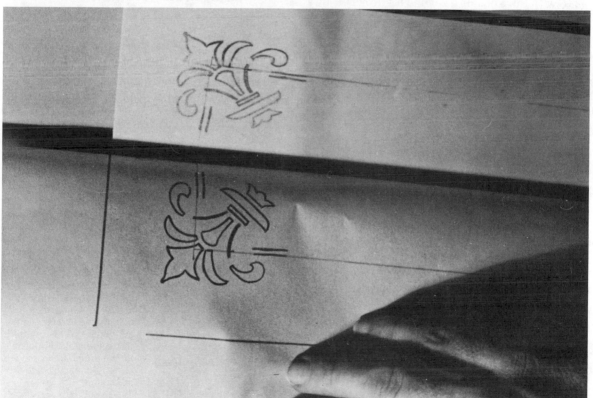

Fig. 4-11. The pencil tracing is peeled back to reveal the transferred design. Notice the registration marks outside the corner motif that were matched with the edge of the glass. Also notice the thin lines intersecting the corner motif. They will act as secondary registration marks and as guides for lines to be cut with a straightedge.

Fig. 4-12. One of the corners has been burnished.

Chapter 7. Because these techniques generally require some practice and insight into the mechanics of designing and obtaining complex multilevel effects in the glass, you must view them with an eye as to why a particular sequence was followed in obtaining the desired result and not merely view them as definitive examples of how every type of design is to be done. Virtually every design has its own sequence of carving steps. In viewing advanced examples, you want to obtain from them the basis by which this sequence is determined. If you are a serious student of this art form, it is not an understatement to say that this learning process will continue for many years, after innumerable carvings and sculptures that come out looking nothing like what you had planned.

simple and should not be viewed as exemplary of the detail or complexity that you can obtain using Levels 1 and 2a in your work. If your main interest is sand-carved glass lies with flat glass, I suggest you also review Project 3, showing the engraved plate with the Rooster design. This project shows an alternative rendering (Level 3a) that is also very easy for the beginning artist or hobbyists to do, yet offers another look and has advantages for those with less-than-professional-level equipment.

If your interest is with more advanced techniques like carving (Level 4) or sculpturing (Level 5), I suggest that you review the advanced projects in

MONOGRAMMED GLASSWARE AND DECANTER

The next projects involve engraving letters in intaglio and high relief. In this case two types of glassware and an antique decanter are used as examples of the wide range of items that can be easily and inexpensively monogrammed through sand carving. Virtually any cylindrical, conical, or flat-faced glass item is very easy to engrave using the techni-

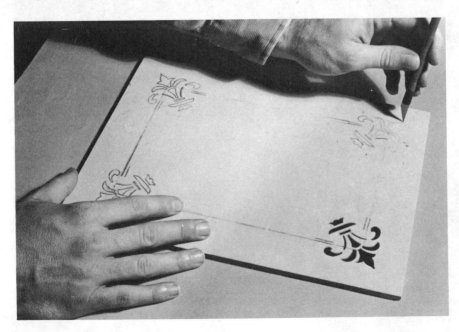

Fig. 4-13. All four corners have been burnished with the design. One corner has been cut out and removed, revealing the glass to be engraved. The glass appears as black here. Note the vertical position of the cutting blade while the design is being cut. Also note the position of the finger holding the cutting blade handle. This allows for the thumb to be used to guide (rotate) the blade during cutting.

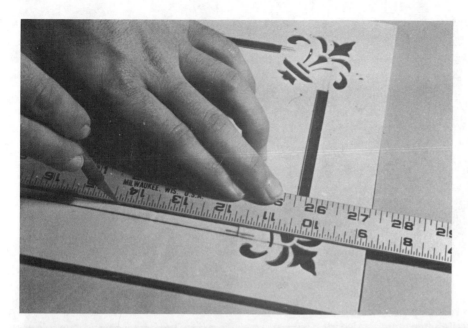

Fig. 4-14. A straightedge is used to make perfect straight cuts using the thin registration lines as guides. All black areas have the stencil removed, and are ready to engrave.

Fig. 4-15. The finished piece.

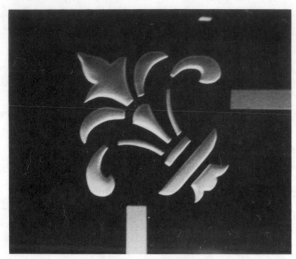

Fig. 4-16. A close up of the corner motif.

ques illustrated in this series of projects.

The concept of high-relief engraving is also introduced in this project, illustrated by the wine glass and the decanter. High relief engraving is very useful where a greater degree of cutting depth is available due to the thickness of the material being decorated, or where opaque materials are to be engraved. Because of the amount of glass that is cut away in high-relief engraving, this method is also very useful when flaws, such as scratches, nicks, or bubbles, must be cut out of an item, as when you are decorating older items that might have some slight surface damage or internal inconsistency. High-relief engraving is also useful when you are decorating such things as ceramics, porcelain, stone of any kind—granite, marble and slate are common—or even bricks.

In working with glassware or any other small items, it cannot be overemphasized how important is proper placement of the design to the overall appearance of the finished piece. (See Figs. 4-17 through 4-24.) Generally speaking, the smaller the item, the more precise the placement must be. Because of the shape of such items as glassware, decanters, and small plates, a variety of reference points are given to the person viewing the finished piece, which makes mistakes in registration very obvious. For example, a monogram or crest motif that is crooked on a glass is very obvious because of the borders created by the top rim of the glass and the sides of the item. For this reason it is very important to pay very close attention to the use of registration marks, placed on the stencil after its application to the glass and prior to the burnishing of the design onto the stencil. It is impossible to give any one standard format for registration lines since there are different types of designs and items that can be engraved. For this reason I have shown a slightly different marking system for each of the following projects.

Registration lines need not be plentiful or complex. All that is necessary is that they act as precise guides for you in placing your artwork (pencil tracing or dry transfer letters or motifs) onto the stencil material. A few lines are generally all that are required. The major mistake made by beginners is that these lines or marks are made hastily or im-

Fig. 4-17. The glasses before engraving.

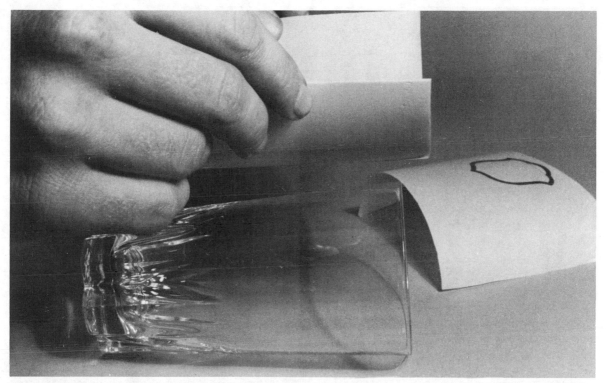

Fig. 4-18. After cleaning the glass with alcohol and water and cutting a small piece of stencil material, all the vinyl backing is removed from the stencil. The stencil is then held between the hands, with the edges upward and the center down toward the surface of the glass. The hands are then lowered slowly, applying the stencil to the glass, starting at the center and proceeding outward to the edge of the stencil.

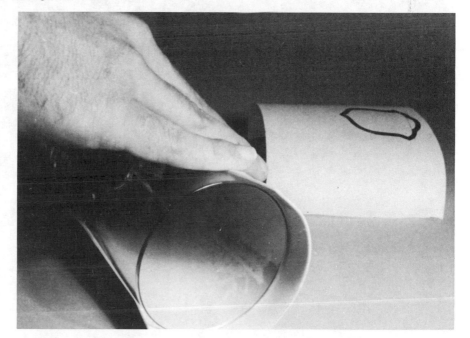

Fig. 4-19. Once the stencil is securely applied, the glass is rolled on any hard surface. Note the prepared pencil tracing of the crest motif in the background.

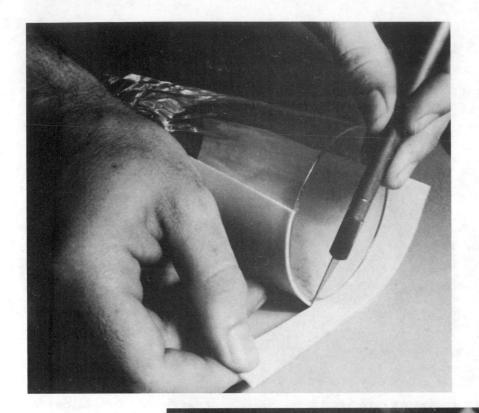

Fig. 4-20. Excessive stencil material is trimmed from the top of the glass allowing the top edge of the glass to act as a reference point in measuring and drawing registration lines.

Fig. 4-21. Drawing of the registration marks using a pen and flexible plastic ruler.

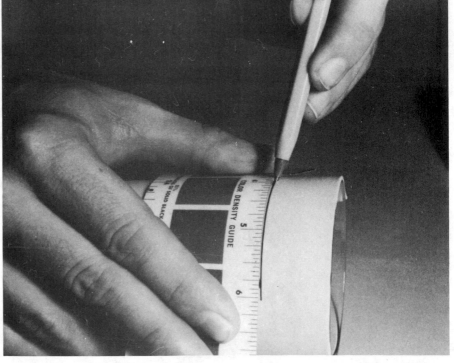

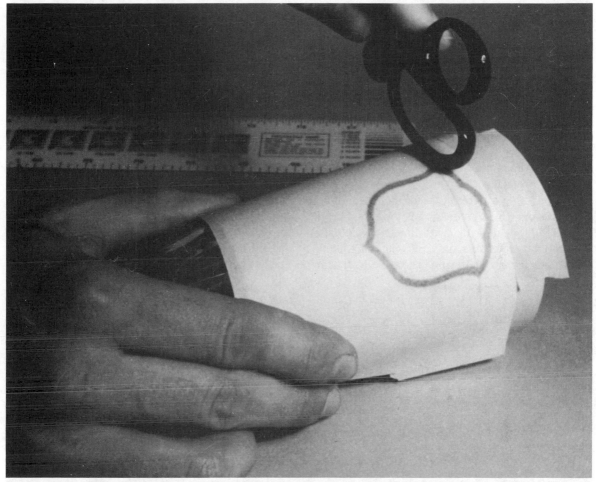

Fig. 4-22. The pencil tracing is placed on the stencil according to the registration marks, taped in place, and burnished onto the stencil using the handle of a pair of scissors.

precisely, thus misguiding the placement of the design.

A good registration mark is generally a line that must intersect with two or more points in the design that is being engraved. A single horizontal and a single vertical line, well drawn, precisely placed, and intersecting two or more points in the design are usually all that you need to ensure that your design is properly placed on the item being engraved. If a number of letters or other complex motifs must be applied in multiple steps (burnishing a border, then applying dry transfer materials, etc.) and you are inexperienced, it is not a bad idea to use the format employed on the decanter project.

In this case graph paper was used, with a number of lines on the graph penciled over, creating the guidelines for placement of the letters. This type of grid is very helpful to anyone who does not have experience with precise registrations or where extreme precision is necessary.

It is also important to note the two types of dry transfer lettering used in these projects. (See Figs 4-25 through 4-34.) On the wine glass, the *W* is burnished directly onto the stencil material from its carrier sheet. In the case of the *JR* on the tea glass, the letters are removed from the carrier sheet then applied to the stencil. Most hobbyists will find the second format easier to work with because it allows for removal and replacement of the letters if a mistake in placement has been made. Those materials that are burnished directly onto the stencil do not allow for removal or replacement. These materials also have the added disadvantage of the distraction and confusion to the eye created by the proximity of all the other letters on the carrier sheet. Note all the other letters around the *W* as it is being burnished onto the stencil on the wine glass. Compare with the relative visibility of the registration lines and overall view of the item in the tea glass project.

In selecting a letter style for monogramming, many people's first inclination is toward "fancy," "detailed," or "delicate, with fine lines." Most of the time this translates into confusing, unreadable, or virtually invisible lettering. Those letters that are

best for monogrammed glass are bold, easy to read, and easy to cut into the stencil. No one is impressed by a monogram that is so fancy that it is unreadable, or is unrecognizable to the point looking like an unwanted mineral stain on the glass. To many people's surprise, two types of letters that tend to be the least suitable for monogramming are Old English and most kinds of Script lettering. Old English is unsuitable because a number of the capital letters are easily confused with each other. Look at the *U, Y, W,* and *V,* and the *I, J,* and *F.* A single, easily recognizable letter in this typeface may be suitable, but put more than one of these letters together, and it is very easy to end up with an unreadable mess.

With Script lettering, the problem is quite different. Often the line work is so fine that the

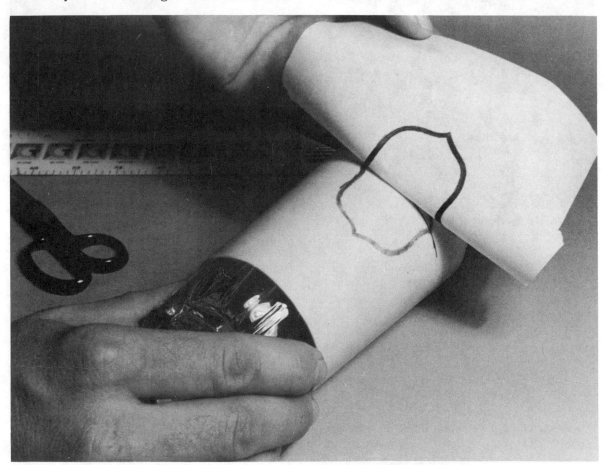

Fig. 4-23. The pencil tracing of the border motif is lifted, showing the transferred design.

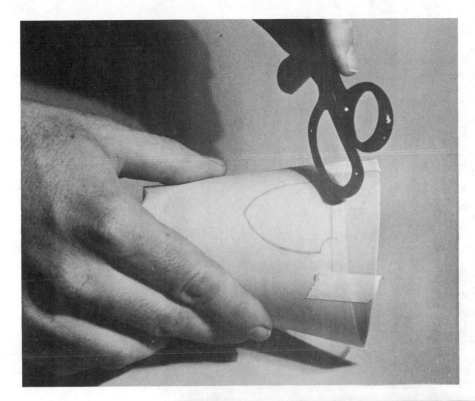

Fig. 4-24. Same procedure on the wine glass.

Fig. 4-25. Cutting out a dry transfer letter for the monogram on the tea glass. Note that the letter is on a transparent carrier sheet with a heavy paper backing. The thin transparent sheet is cut using the cutting blade and lifted off the paper backing.

Fig. 4-26. The "J" has been positioned onto the stencil and the "R" is now being put on, guided by the registration marks.

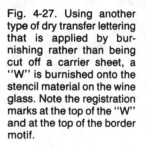

Fig. 4-27. Using another type of dry transfer lettering that is applied by burnishing rather than being cut off a carrier sheet, a "W" is burnished onto the stencil material on the wine glass. Note the registration marks at the top of the "W" and at the top of the border motif.

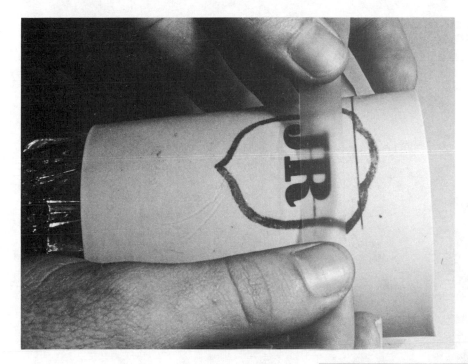

Fig. 4-28. After the letters have been applied, clear tape is applied over the letter to hold the letters in place during cutting.

monogram is virtually invisible after engraving. This combined with the difficulty in precisely cutting line work 1/32 to 1/16 inch in width makes script monograms less than satisfying for most hobbyists. Such letter styles as Souvenir Medium, Souvenir Demi, Souvenir Bold, Windsor Elongated, or Korrinna are excellent. They are easy to cut, they engrave well, and they are easy to read once they are engraved. As a general rule, serif typefaces are more attractive than sans serif styles.

The decanter is included as an example of the many high-quality items that can be found at estate sales, flea markets, and antique dealers for a fraction of their current retail replacement value. This decanter was purchased for $.25, and could cost several hundred dollars if a comparable contemporary item were to be found. This particular piece is fine lead crystal and has very thick walls suitable for high-relief engraving (see Figs. 4-35 through 4-43), and virtually every surface has been hand-cut and polished. Such "plain" items tend to be held in low regard by antique dealers and collectors of antique cut glass and are available for next to nothing. The plate used in the engraving of the Rooster motif later in this chapter and the small

Fig. 4-29. Both glasses with stencils, letters, and clear tape applied ready for cutting.

Fig. 4-30. A single cut is made around the border motif of the wine glass.

Fig. 4-31. A single cut is made around the letter "W" on the wine glass.

Fig. 4-32. After cutting, the rubber stencil has been removed from those areas which are to be engraved. Note that a single cut around the border of the "W" was all that was necessary to remove the crest, leaving the "W" (now with the black transfer letter removed) completely surrounded by the crest design that is to be engraved. Note that a double cut was necessary to remove the line work border from around the "JR" in order to engrave the outline of the crest design. All areas that appear black in the photograph are exposed glass, ready to be engraved.

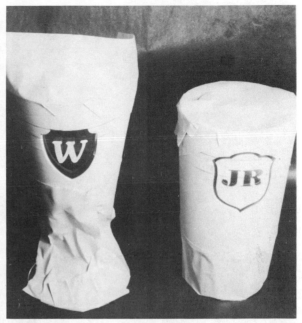

Fig. 4-33. Masking tape applied in order to prevent "overblast" from etching the stem, bottom, or inside of the glassware.

Fig. 4-34. The finished pieces. Note how the black areas in Fig. 4-32 are all now white and engraved. The "W" is clear and high in relation to the engraved background forming the crest motif. The crest on the tea glass has been outlined with a heavy engraved line and the letters "JR" have been cut into the glass.

vase used in the advanced projects in Chapter 7 were all purchased from these sources. The most I paid for any of these items was $1.00! These are important and virtually untapped sources for engraving blanks for the hobbyist or skilled amateur.

When you are looking at this type of item with engraving in mind, it is most important to remember that many flaws can be engraved out of the item. Thus, scratches, nicks, bubbles, etc. become meaningless (except in negotiating the asking price downward) with regard to the final appearance or usefulness of the item. Simply design your engraving so these characteristics are blasted out of the glass. High-relief work is good for this because of the amount of glass removed and the

Fig. 4-35. The decanter before engraving.

flexibility in designing a background format that covers all the surface flaws. In pointing out a severe scratch or nick in the glass, you can obtain the item at a fraction of its marked price, which is already a fraction of the retail value of a contemporary replacement. Vases, decanters, bowls, and plates will be the most common items of this kind that you will find. Matched sets of glassware that are uncut or otherwise suitable for engraving are quite uncommon. Contemporary glassware is reasonable enough in price to use for engraving.

MULTILEVEL ENGRAVING/ETCHING

This project will demonstrate how to obtain multilevel engraving and etching combinations using engraved line work and refrosting, which I called Level 3 work in Chapter 1. (See Figs. 4-44 through 4-57.) This is one of the easiest ways to obtain multilevel effects on glass and is a very useful method for the beginning student or artist to learn to manipulate the various effects obtainable through

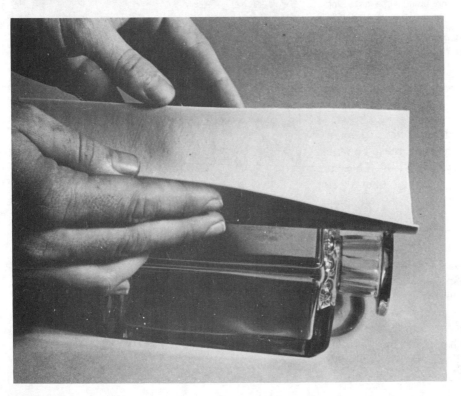

Fig. 4-36. The stencil is applied to one side.

Fig. 4-37. Another shot of Fig. 4-36.

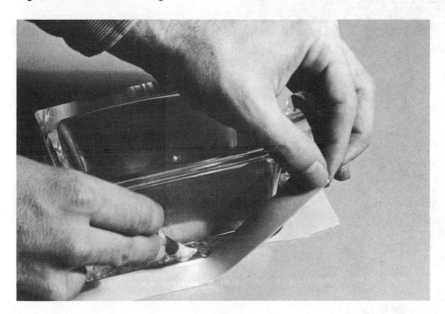

Fig. 4-38. Excess stencil is trimmed from the edge.

Fig. 4-39. Stencil has been applied and trimmed from both sides. A set of registration marks is burnished onto the stencil on each side.

Fig. 4-40. The pencil tracing of the registration marks is lifted showing the transfer of the grid. Black, dry transfer letters were then applied using the lines and guides. The letters were then taped in place and cut out. After cutting of the letter, a single line was cut using a straightedge, forming the border of the background to be engraved.

Fig. 4-41. The decanter is ready for blasting. Note the masking tape used to cover all exposed areas.

of the pencil lines of the design to be engraved. Look at the border around the "JR" monogram in the last project as an example. The heavy line was cut on the outside edge and along the inside edge so the line making up the crest motif could be removed for engraving. I used the same idea for this project, except the design is considerably more complex. After the line work was cut and removed, all line work was engraved into the glass. All the stencil material within the design was then removed and lightly surface-etched, creating a second level to the decoration. Thus I ended up with engraved line work and flat etched areas filling out the design.

This stencil breakdown is excellent for the individual who wants to design original decorations, but lacks the opportunity to experiment with professional-level equipment to acquire carving or sculpturing skills, or who does not want to spend the time necessary to learn how to design with these more advanced techniques. Through engraved line work and etching, virtually any beginner can render countless designs from a wide range of sources, if he can generate an outline and some in-

sand carving. It is also one of the most efficient ways of decorating because the amount of glass that must be blasted away in the engraving stage can be quite insignificant in relation to the overall size of the decoration. Simply outline a design with engraved line work, then etch everything within the line work, and you have a multilevel decoration. Nothing could be simpler. Additionally, the next step in complexity, Level 3b requires nothing more than controlling the etching so that shading effects are obtained. Thus a single stencil breakdown will work for two very different looks on the glass.

This project also illustrates another example of a glass item found at a flea market for a fraction of its replacement retail value. This devilled egg plate was purchased for $1.00, and through engraving was made into a one-of-a-kind gift for a friend.

In obtaining engraved line work, it is important to remember that you must cut a line on both sides

Fig 4-42 Another view of the masking tape.

Fig. 4-43. The finished decanter engraved in high relief.

terior detail lines indicating the major structures within the design. Simply engrave the lines and refrost all the areas within the line work. That's all there is to it.

This type of rendering is also very useful for the individual who wants to render buildings in glass. Because most buildings easily suggest a line work rendering, they are particularly easy to depict in this way. Thus your home or cabin by the lake can become the subject for your own original engraving. This type of rendering is also very useful for the person who is decorating a piece of flat glass with a border motif, such as a Victorian border from a Dover Publications Book. If the only compressor you have available is quite small (1 to 2 hp) and your glass is quite large (24 to 30 + inches: one dimension), you should consider engraving the outlines of the segments making up your border design, then

Fig. 4-44. Deviled egg plate prior to engraving.

refrosting those areas within the engraved line work. In this way you have significantly decreased the amount of glass you must remove in order to obtain highlights at the edges of your border segments, also reducing your blasting time and the amount of abrasive you must have to complete the project.

This is an excellent way of producing a lot of *look* efficiently and easily. Unlike carving and sculpturing, which can result in a lot of surprises for beginning designers, it is almost impossible to make a mistake with engraved line work and solid refrosting.

This project is also important because I did not use registration marks on the stencil as guides for placement of the pencil tracing prior to burnishing it onto the stencil. The reason is very simple. This design is a nonsymmetrical, odd-shaped design. Precise and mechanical placement of this type of design within a precise format often results in registration which may be "ruler perfect" but which looks unbalanced to the eye. For this reason this design was placed on the stencil and moved around until a balanced fit was found. By this I mean that the outermost aspects of the design (feet, tail, comb) were balanced as equally as possible in relation to their proximity to the round border on the bottom of the plate. After a suitable placement

Fig. 4-45. Applying the stencil, just like for Project #6. Because of the small size of the stencil material, all of the vinyl backing has been removed prior to beginning application to the plate. It is important to remember that the adhesive side of the stencil must never touch itself. If this happens, the stencil will be deformed and useless when pulled apart.

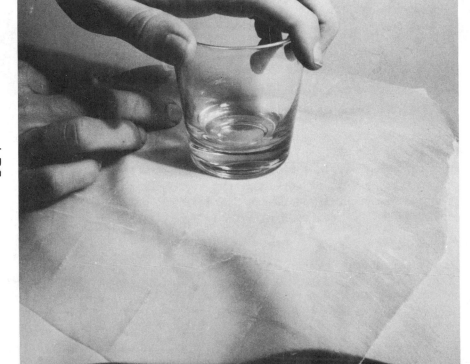

Fig. 4-46. The stencil is burnished onto the glass using wax paper and the bottom of a glass.

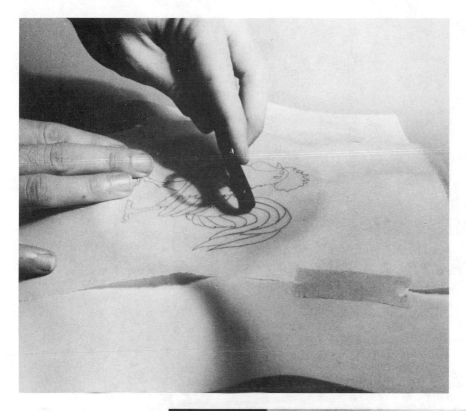

Fig. 4-47. Rather than using registration marks, the pencil tracing was placed on the stencil by "guestimation" then confirmed through ruler measure-4CELments. This is a common way of registering odd shaped designs, which may look out of place if registered by precise mechanical measurements. After placement, the design is taped into place and burnished onto the stencil using the handle of a pair of scissors.

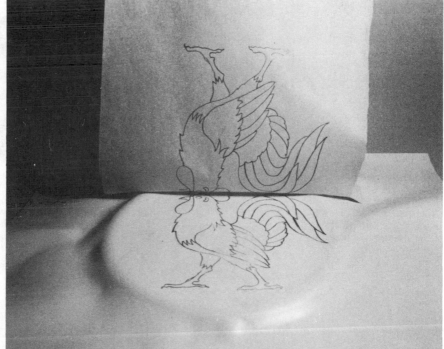

Fig. 4-48. The pencil tracing is lifted, revealing the transferred design.

Fig. 4-49. Close up of the pencil design on the stencil prior to cutting, show the key points of the design used in estimating proper placement of the design onto the glass. Key points are the feet, tail, and comb. The distances between these characteristics were balanced between the circular border of the bottom of the plate.

Fig. 4-50. The design has now been cut on both sides of all pencil lines, allowing for complete removal of the pencil drawing, which is shown being pulled out. The heavy black lines indicate areas where the stencil has been removed. Compare with the look of the feet and tail, which are shown being removed.

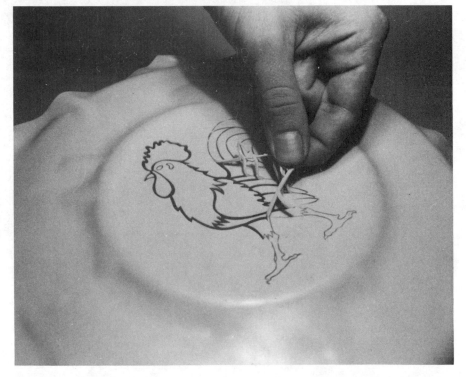

Fig. 4-51. All of the pencil line work has been cut from the stencil and removed. Note the removed stencil material on the left.

was found, a ruler was used to measure the distances between these characteristics and the outside border. A slight adjustment was then made, resulting in an eye-pleasing placement of the design.

PORCELAIN PLATE

In this project an inexpensive porcelain plate was engraved in a single-level design of a peacock motif traced from an enlargement of a design from a dry-transfer lettering catalog. (See Figs. 4-58 through 4-67.) This project introduces working with opaque materials, which can include virtually any type of ceramic material, various types of stone (granite, marble, slate) and a variety of opaque glass. It is important to remember when you are working with opaque materials that the finished design is viewed from the same side that it is worked on. This is the

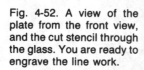

Fig. 4-52. A view of the plate from the front view, and the cut stencil through the glass. You are ready to engrave the line work.

Fig. 4-53. Another view of the design with all stencil material in the line work removed. It has been back lit to illuminate the cut and removed areas.

Fig. 4-54. The line work has now been engraved. All of the stencil material within the design must be removed for refrosting.

Fig. 4-55. All stencil material within the design has now been removed and is ready for refrosting. All black areas within the design are now clear glass that has been exposed for refrosting. Note how the light creates highlights on the engraved line work.

opposite of most clear glass work (except high-relief engraving and carving), in which the finished design is viewed though the glass; i.e., in reverse.

This particular design was chosen for a number of reasons, one of which is because it is an example of the literally hundreds of designs available in camera-ready form in the dry-transfer format shown in the second project. This design comes in the same format as the *JR* lettering. Secondly, this design demonstrates the use of high-relief characteristics (those areas within the design which have not been cut into the porcelain) and intaglio cutting (those areas which have been cut into the porcelain) in order to obtain a variety of effects in a single-step engraving.

Note that the actual body of the peacock (head, neck, body) was cut into the plate, and the details in the tail were left in high-relief. The principle here is to engrave into the material those parts of the design that you want to suggest form (the body in this case) and all the background within the border of the design, leaving small interior details in high-relief.

Fig. 4-56. The interior of the design has now been refrosted and all other stencil material removed, showing the completed design. Note how the engraved line work contrasts with the flat surfaces that have been etched, creating a two-level effect.

Fig. 4-57. The completed piece.

Fig. 4-58. The original camera-ready art we used as the basis for the design.

Fig. 4-59. The simplified tracing used for the design on the plate.

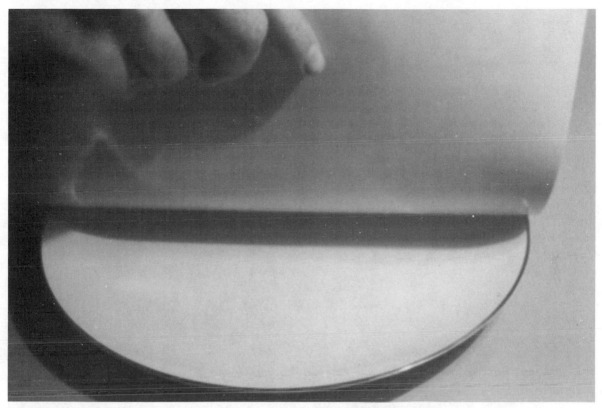

Fig. 4-60. After cleaning the surface of the plate, cutting a piece of stencil sufficient to cover the entire plate, and removing all of the vinyl backing, one side of the stencil is held high in one hand while the other hand applies the stencil to the surface of the plate with a slow "walking" motion of the fingers.

The result should be that at least 40 to 50 percent of the area within your design has been cut into the opaque material, resulting in a visible and easily recognizable engraving. Nothing is more frustrating than to put the time and effort into a project only to realize the result is virtually invisible because of a lack of engraved surface.

In porcelain or any other ceramic material, a visible and recognizable result is of greater importance because of the potential for the engraved piece to be decorated with colored glazes (ceramic enamels). Thus, a well-designed and -executed engraving is only the beginning of obtaining a truly unique piece. The arts and crafts stores that stock porcelain blanks like the one used in this project often have the materials and facility (high-fire kilns) necessary for this additional work. They will either do the work according to your instructions or will teach you how to do the work yourself.

The tracing of this design also demonstrates a principle that is useful to learn early if you plan to continue to design your own engravings or work from more indirect sources for designs. In previous projects, most of the areas that were to be engraved into the glass or other material were black (penciled) in the tracing. After the stencil was cut, these black areas were removed for engraving. Note that in this design the body of the peacock is black and was removed for engraving, and that the interior details of the tail were also blacked in these parts of the stencil were not removed, however, and so where left unengraved and high in relation to the engraved background. This is an example of inconsistency and wasted time in penciling the tracing.

The idea is for you to break out of the concept that only black areas of your design can be

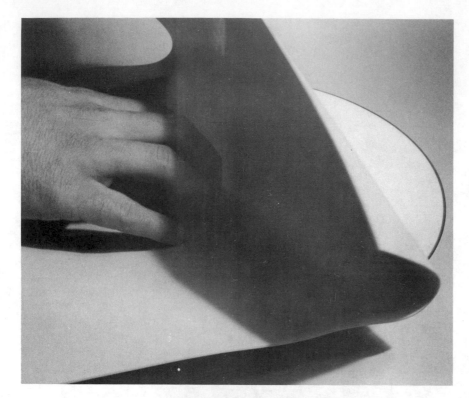

Fig. 4-61. Another view of applying the stencil.

Fig. 4-62. The stencil is burnished into place using wax paper and the bottom of a glass.

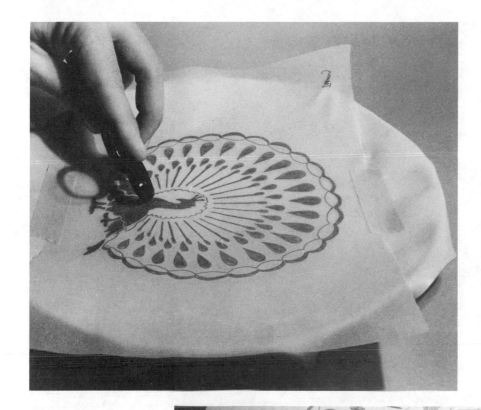

Fig. 4-63. The pencil tracing is burnished onto the stencil, after placement by "guestimation." Just like the chicken on the egg plate, placement is confirmed by ruler measurements. Note the tracing is taped in place prior to burnishing.

Fig. 4-64. The pencil tracing is peeled back, revealing the burnished design on the stencil.

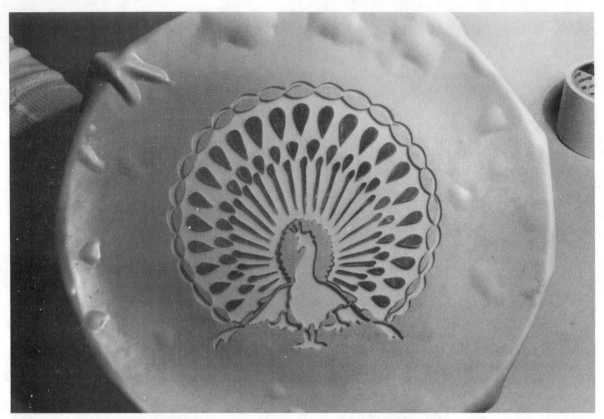

Fig. 4-65. The stencil has been cut, and all the areas to be engraved have been removed. Note that some areas removed were penciled black, while others were not.

engraved, and that all areas that are to be engraved must be penciled black in your tracing. You should begin to view your tracing as a cutting guide only, keeping in mind what you are going to remove and engrave. A little bit of planning can save hours of needless tracing. By looking at my inconsistent example, you should be able to see how I could have reduced the area I blacked in. Outlines of each discrete section making up the design are all that should be required. Look at the rendering used for the multilevel Rooster design in the third project. That type of outline should be all you need for virtually any design you will ever engrave or carve.

You will find this a valuable way of thinking about engraving designs when you are looking at design sources, whether they are camera ready or in a more indirect form. When you are looking at camera-ready art, do not automatically assume that all black areas must be engraved. Can the areas around the black areas be engraved for a unique effect? Can the black areas be outlined (like the Rooster) then refrosted within those lines? Will a tracing of the edges of the black areas result in enough guidelines for your stencil cutting? These are some of the questions you should consider when you create your own projects. The idea is to not allow the reference artwork to dictate the type of rendering in your engravings, and to spend as little time as possible tracing your intended design. Remember, a few minutes of planning can save hours of tracing and will help you develop skill in imagining a variety of renderings of a single design.

Keep this in mind as you review the Comparative Designs in Chapter 3, remembering that each rendering was generated from identical line work tracings of the original design.

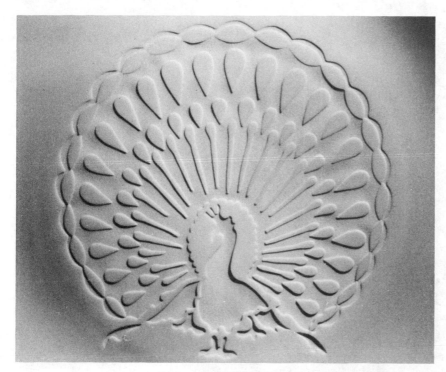

Fig. 4-66. Close-up of the finished engraving.

Fig. 4-67. The completed plate ready for glazing or inlay.

Suggested Designs
for Your Projects

5

In this chapter are included over 70 camera-ready designs for your own projects. The designs will vary in degree of difficulty, but there is something for every level of sand carver, from the first-time glass artist to the skilled professional. It is important to remember that the degree of difficulty is generally determined by the type of rendering you are making, rather than by the design itself. In other words, just because a given design suggests sculpturing or another advanced technique, there is no need to render it that way if you are just learning about sand carving. If you are familiar with the levels of renderings mentioned in Chapter 1, and have read Chapter 3 illustrating the comparative designs, you should have no problem in determining how to trace and use these designs in such a way that your very first projects come out beautifully.

When you are looking at these designs, it is important to remember that it is perfectly valid to simplify a design to fit the size you want to make and the item you want to engrave. If a plant is shown with 20 leaves, and your stained glass window only has room for 12 leaves, fine, just trace off the 12 leaves you need for your project. If a bird's wing has 30 feathers, and you are making a small mirror using the design and only have room for 8 or 10 feathers, just trace what you need. By using these designs as beginning points for your projects, you should find this collection a limitless source for your own work.

Because of the popularity of etched mirrors, I have included a number of border designs specifically designed for mirrors. Some of these designs are quite detailed, while others are very simple.

When you are looking at a detailed or complex border motif, you should keep in mind that you need not reproduce every curve and line in order to make a very beautiful item. The attractiveness of an etched mirror often lies with the "effect" of etching the surface and not with the complexity or details of the design. Simplify, simplify, simplify. Do not let yourself be intimidated by curliques and fancy line work. Such details often require that more time be spent in making your project, and do not necessarily add to the degree of difficulty in executing the actual sand carving. With a little practice you will undoubtedly surprise yourself with what you can make in a few hours of tracing and stencil cutting. All you have to do then is take your prepared mirror to the local monument maker's shop, and for a few dollars you should be able to get it deep cut. The same thing goes for glassware, clear plate glass, flashed stained glass, porcelain, or virtually anything else you will want to make.

In looking at most of these designs, you might assume that the black areas are to be cut into the glass and the white areas are to be left clear (or silvered in the case of a mirror). This is not always the case, but it is an excellent way to begin looking at potential designs for your own work. If a design is made up of very thin black line work, with mostly white areas within the thin outlines, you might consider rendering that type of design like the third project in Chapter 4. This will give a very sophisticated multilevel look. This style of rendering can be done by the first-time hobbyist.

The idea is for you take a little time to read the introductory chapters on technique and the chapter on beginning projects, so that you can begin to design your own original renderings of the designs I have included. In this way your projects are truly your own and are not simply duplicates of the furnished designs.

If the size of the design you wish to reproduce is not right for your project, you can increase its size by use of an opaque projector or by taking this book to a typesetting house and asking them to give you a "positive paper print" in the size you need. Because these designs are camera ready, they are in a format which is designed for reproduction through standard graphic processes. Size reductions are also available from these same sources. In this way you can trace the design in exactly the size you wish to sand-carve.

The letter code next to each design denotes its source, as follows:

A) *Victorian Stencils for Design and Decoration,* by Edmund V. Gillon, Jr. Dover Publications.
B) *Art Nouveau & Early Art Deco Type & Design from the Roman Scherer Catalogue,* Edited by Theodore Menten. Dover Publications.
C) *Floral Designs,* Designed by Ed Sibbett, Jr. Dover Publications.
D) *Chinese Folk Designs,* by W.M. Hawley Dover Publications.
E) *The Mucha Poster Coloring Book,* by Ed Sibbett, Jr. Dover Publications.
F) *Treasury of Chinese Design Motifs,* by Joseph D'Addetta. Dover Publications.
G) *Cartouches and Decorative Small Frames,* Edited by Edmund Gillon, Jr. Dover Publications.
H) *Harter's Picture Archive for Collage and Illustration,* Edited by Jim Harter. Dover Publications.
I) *Art Nouveau, An Anthology of Design and Illustration from The Studio,* selected by Edmund Gillon, Jr. Dover Publications.
J) Original Designs, by Barbara Behun.

PRECIOUS WENTLETRAP

J

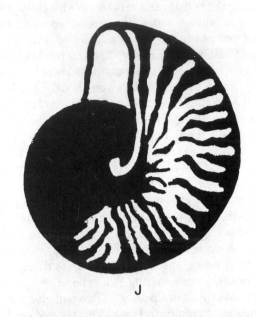

J

J

CHAMBERED NAUTILUS

J

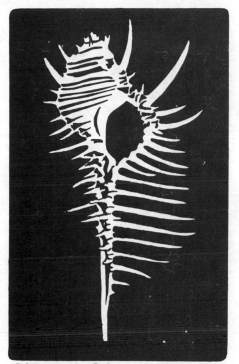 J

VENUS COMB MUREX

 J

 J

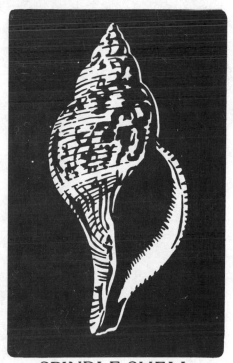 J

 J

SPINDLE SHELL

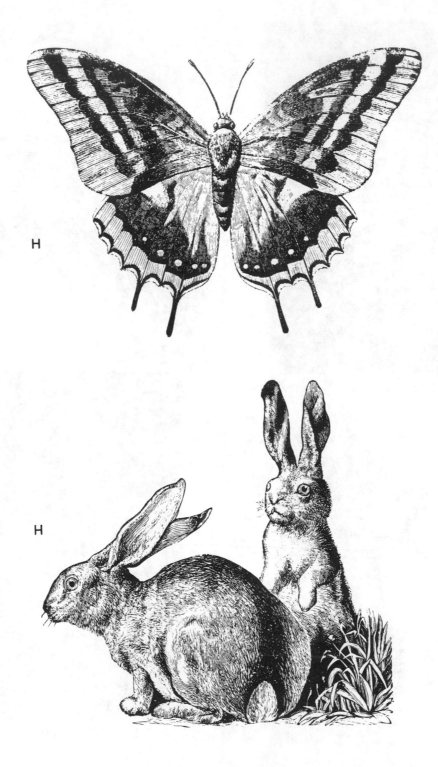

H

H

H

H

H

II

A

A

A

A

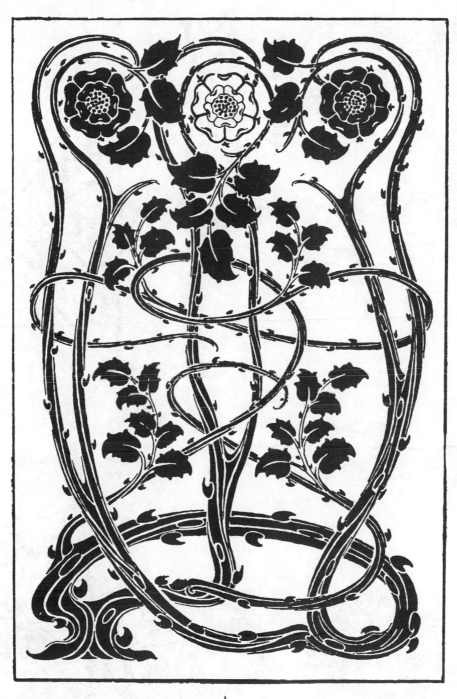

I

G

A

C

C

c

c

c

J

J

A

J

J

J

J

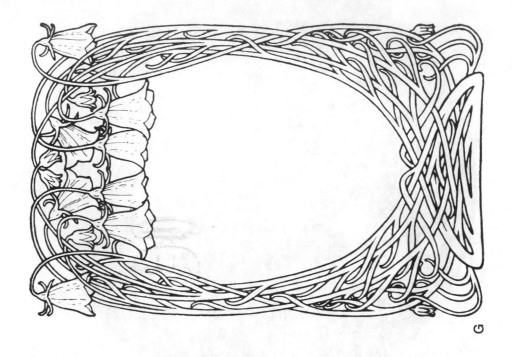

G

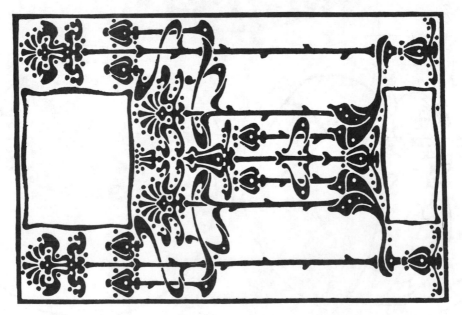

H

116

G

G

J

B

J

B

B

B

I

I

B

B

119

J

J

J

J

D

D

D

D

D

121

E

E

F

F

G

E

F

F

123

PAT

J

A

J

J D

J

J

A

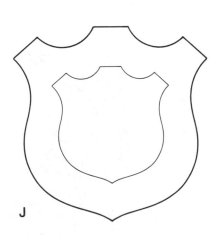

J

A

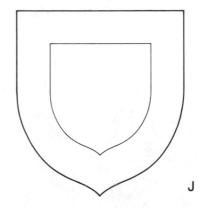

J

MARY

J

T**H**E

J

DJW

J

A

H

126

Additional Sources for Designs and Further Study  6

In this chapter are a number of suggestions for sources of designs for your own original sand-carved glass. Most of these sources are much more secondary than camera-ready art, although I do suggest additional sources of designs in that format. For the serious student of engraved, carved, and sculptured glass and crystal, I offer review of the copper wheel engraving tradition of Czechoslovakia over the last 300 years and make special note of other trend-setting or definitive work of the nineteenth and twentieth centuries in other European countries. Reviewing this previous work will help you to gain many insights into the sculptural potential of glass and crystal. The idea is not for this previous work to be copied in your sand carving, but to illustrate styles of glass sculpturing and to illustrate the insights demonstrated by the most gifted designer/artists that have worked with developing the potential of this medium.

This chapter contains sources that would be of interest to the hobbyist who wants to develop his designs beyond that shown in Chapter 5, yet does not want to spend many hours in the library. I also offer starting points for the serious student of engraved glass and the skilled professional to widen their familiarity with the previous work of the undisputed masters of this art form. Regardless of your skill level or interest in further study, this chapter offers a number of alternatives to the designs contained in this book.

CAMERA-READY ART

One of the most common misconceptions concerning sand-carved glass is that you must be an artist or be able to draw in order to make attractive and useful items. Nothing could be further from the truth. Many very attractive and useful projects are available to the person who can hardly draw a straight line with a ruler! All that is needed, in addition to the basic materials and access to the equipment, is a familiarity with the basic vocabulary of sand-carved glass (Levels 1 through 5), an ability to trace, and most importantly, good reference materials. This chapter tells you where to look for good reference, and where in fact, many professionals obtain their ideas.

While it would be accurate to say that virtually any previously made piece of artwork could serve as a reference for your designs, that would not be very helpful. What you need are specific books, styles of design, or items that lend themselves to interpretation into a stencil breakdown consistent with your skill level and available equipment.

The easiest reference material for beginners tends to be black-and-white camera-ready art. Most often the black areas of the design are cut into the glass, and the white areas outside the design are left clear. Solid refrosting or etching within the borders of the black areas can easily be added, like the third project in Chapter 4, with the resulting multilevel effects. This type of reference artwork is available from a number of sources, but the most common are the Dover Publications series of designs, which includes collections of Victorian border stencils (see Chapter 7), frame and cartouche designs, design devices, and countless other designs and motifs collected from particular periods of history or cultural backgrounds. Virtually every professional flat glass sand carver has a few Dover books in their reference library. Some of the titles I have collected over the years are listed later in this chapter, and a complete listing of Dover books can be obtained at your local bookstore or by writing Dover Publications, 180 Varick St., New York, NY 10014. When you write to the publisher, you should refer to the "Dover Pictorial Archive Series," since this series contains most of the titles that cover period and cultural designs.

Additionally, your local commercial artist supply store will have a wealth of designs for you. These stores sell supplies for commercial illustrators, architects, painters, etc. They carry a full line of dry-transfer lettering, which were used to obtain perfect letters on the monogrammed glassware illustrated in Chapter 4. The same companies that make these materials also make an overwhelming number of copyright-free borders, designs, and motifs in the same transfer format. The range of designs is far too broad to go over here, but if you want just about anything in a camera-ready, black-and-white format, they will have it ready to transfer to your rubber matte.

Because of the size of some of the renderings, you may have a problem, but since they are camera ready, you can have enlargements made at any typesetting house for a few dollars or can project them easily with an opaque projector. These materials can be selected from catalogues that the dealers keep on hand. The designs are sold on sheets, each of which contains a number of designs. With two or three sheets you could easily compose dozens of projects. The easiest way to find dealers in your area is to go through the Yellow Pages of your telephone book, and look under "Artist's Supplies" (not "Arts and Crafts"), call those firms listed, and ask if they carry dry-transfer lettering. If they carry the lettering, they will also carry the other design materials as well. While you are in the store, inquire if they have books of *clip art* which are collections of more copyright-free designs employed by professional illustrators in composing advertising art of all kinds. Most of it is also camera ready; thus, it is easily enlarged to the size you need for your project.

STAINED GLASS PATTERN BOOKS

Another source of designs that many stained glass artists and hobbyists will already have, is stained glass window pattern books. The designs in these books are most often very simple breakdowns of figurative designs or border motifs made up of bold black line work, similar to my rendering of the Rooster on the glass plate. The bold lines indicate the leading or metal used to hold the individual stained glass pieces in place. For sand carving, these bold lines can indicate several things, depending on the level of your work. You can engrave these lines and refrost all the areas within the lines, in which case you have engraved line work and solid refrosting. Many of these designs will also offer the opportunity for shaded refrosting, like the rose and butterfly renderings shown in the comparative renderings in Chapter 3.

If you wish to experiment with carving and sculpturing, these designs offer that opportunity. Use the heavy lines to indicate the single cuts in your stencil and determine the sequence of removal of each section, and you will have a carving. It is important to remember when you are working with this particular design source that included in the design are lines delineating how the background is broken up for inclusion of stained glass. For sand carving, you should ignore these and leave the background clear or use them as a guide for incorporating stained glass around your sand-carved glass. In this way a stained glass pattern book has provided you with a sand carving design and a layout for a sand-carved glass/stained-glass window combination.

These designs furnish you with the necessary line work to begin to experiment with various techniques and levels of work, which is very helpful if you are lacking in drawing skills or training. By reviewing these books, you will begin to see how seemingly complex subjects can be broken down into discrete sections that work together in creating the illusion of the subject depicted. Remember, these renderings will have no color and no shading of any kind. Those are the two things you will need to learn to remove from your stencil breakdowns for sand carving, even though shading and form will be given to the design in its final rendering on the glass. Allow the line work in these renderings to act as stencil-cutting guides, and let your imagination determine how the design will be rendered into the glass.

ART FORMS

If you are interested in working from more indirect sources of design, the hunting ground is extremely broad with respect to the types of items or work that will be of help. It is most important, though, to look at designs and renderings that will lend themselves to sand-carved glass. Otherwise, attempting to translate a design from one medium to that of sand-carved glass can be quite frustrating until some degree of skill is obtained. For this reason I will go over particular art forms and periods of design that should be helpful.

Because sand-carved glass is a sculptural medium, it is only logical that other sculptures should be helpful. This idea is both obvious and misleading, however. It is quite difficult to take a three-dimensional sculptural work of art and translate it into line work for stencil cutting. Bas-relief renderings are useful, however, and someone interested in developing carving and sculpturing skill can gain excellent practice by working from them. When you are considering bas-reliefs, it is most important not to limit yourself to classical, modeled, marble reliefs contained in most art history books. You should also look at engraved gemstones (listed under "glyptic arts" in your library) from the Greek and Roman period and more importantly at the work of the Czech and German engravers of the seventeenth through nineteenth centuries. Contemporary work coming out of the German town of Idar-Oberstein would also be of interest. Ancient carved stone, used for embellishing the walls of buildings, should also be of interest. The work of the ancient Egyptians, Babylonians, Greeks, and Mayans show an excellent technique of modeling and obtaining a great deal of form with a minimum of line work. Repousse metal work, particularly jewelry, is an excellent source for sculptural designs, as illustrated in one of the advanced projects in Chapter 7. Any ancient culture working with gold would also have done repousse work. The work of the Scythians in what is now Russia, should be of particular interest. An excellent source for very refined design within a very small format are the Japanese sword guards of the seventeenth to nineteenth centuries. The skill of execution and layout, required because of the limited space and bas-relief renderings, are exceptional and are easily adapted to circular and octagonal formats for glass. Although these types of renderings may be too advanced for many students or artisans, virtually everyone interested in advanced techniques can benefit from looking at them.

Oriental Art

If you are interested more in engraved linework and refrosting, I suggest you look at a wide variety of Oriental arts. Virtually anything that is Chinese or Japanese will show great skill in the layout or composition of the piece while incorporating a flow or movement between the elements of the design that is particularly applicable for glass. Too often compositions with birds or plant life can end up looking very static or frozen on the glass because of the fact that you only have a limited range of expression using line work and etching. Therefore the positioning of the individual elements of a design is most important. Look at the silhouettes and arrangement of the elements of a composition. Although you will not be able to duplicate the detail or color contained in the original, these are excellent sources for well-conceived, well-balanced compositions. Remember, you will be simplifying to a great degree when you are applying the vocabulary I have gone over.

An Oriental art form that is particularly adapted to a stencil breakdown, to the point that you could virtually trace the line work and have a design ready to burnish onto your rubber and cut, is *cloisonne enameling*. This technique of enameling involves the attaching of thin wires to a metal base (most often a vase, bowl, plate, or other decorative accessory) so that discrete sections, known as *cloisons*, are formed. These sections are then filled with enamel of different colors, resulting in the desired design. These wires form the line work of your tracing. Look at Project 3 in Chapter 4 and imagine colored enamels put into the areas that were etched after the line work was engraved. These are the areas that would be filled with enamels in a cloisonne. Thus, when you look at a cloisonne rendering, you would see a beautifully colored rooster.

Don't let the color or beauty of the original blind you to the fine line work necessary to execute this art form. Ignore the color and trace the wires in the design. the result will surprise you. You can then engrave and etch like my project or carve the design by engraving each section of the design in sequence, as illustrated the Rooster design in Fig. 3-15.

Czech Copper-Wheel Engraving

For the serious student of carved glass, it would be very helpful to research the copper-wheel-engraved crystal produced in Europe over the past 300 years. Because of the degree of control inherent in copper-wheel engraving, it is the technique that is most able to demonstrate the sculptural potential of glass or crystal. Because the rich tradition of copper-wheel engraving as practiced in Czechoslovakia (Bohemia and Silesia in particular) has established the standard by which all other work of this kind is measured, I will give a brief historical overview of it. This information should be of help to anyone wishing to investigate further.

Beginning in the late 1500s, Prague became the most important center of Renaissance Mannerism. This brought a tremendous influx of artists, craftsmen, scholars, and alchemists. With them came the Miseroni and Saracchi families of Milan, Italy. The members of these families were among the leading gemstone cutters and engravers of the period. In this climate of official patronage, combined with the presence of leading engravers the native traditions of engraving and glass decorating began a long and illustrious history that continues today.

One of the premier figures of this period was Caspar Lehman, credited by some with reinventing engraving on glass, and with being the first European to engrave on hollow objects such as goblets and vases. Lehman was a classically trained gemstone engraver who combined the traditions of the northern engravers of Munich and Dresden with that of the southern Milanese. He combined his apprenticeship in the northern cities with professional practice in Prague during a period of influence of the southern gem engraving tradition.

While it is true that historians often grant importance to those figures who can best be documented and this is obviously the case with Lehman, he nonetheless represents the forefront of work of this kind from this period. Other early engravers of note during this period are George Schwanhardt the Elder, David Engelhard (from Nuremburg), Friedrich Winter, and George Schindler (from Jablonec).

During the nineteenth and twentieth centuries, the engraving tradition of Czechoslovakia reached new heights both stylistically and technically. The range of personal and regional styles of technique, subject matter, and items that were engraved was exceptionally broad and reflected deep understanding of the material and its sculptural potential. Noteworthy engravers of the nineteenth century include the Piesche family, Franz Hansel, Franz Gottstein, Eduard Benda, A.H. Mattoni, A.H. Pfeiffer, Emanuel Hoffman, F.A. Pelikan, August Bohm, and Karl Pfofl.

One engraver, Dominik Biemann, deserves special mention. This particular glass artist is generally regarded as one of the finest glass engravers in history. Specializing in portraits generally made from live sittings, Biemann's work demonstrates a control of form and sensitivity to both subject and the material being engraved that is rarely matched in glass or any other medium. Like any noteworthy portrait, his work goes far beyond merely depicting the subject; it captures something of the individual.

During the twentieth century, the innovative leadership of the Czech engraving tradition has continued to grow artistically and technically. Introducing the concept of freelance artist/designers working with glass factories, the Czechs have updated traditional styles and concepts in a way that has redefined cut and engraved glass and crystal. Innovative themes, styles of rendering, and technical mastery, combined with the deepest insight into the character of the material and its potential, make the work of such artists as Josef Drahonosky, Haroslav Horejc, Frantisek Kysela, Jaroslav Benda, and V.H. Benda an indispensable source for study. The latest in contemporary engraving and carving continues to build on the traditional respect and sensitivity demonstrated by centuries of glass work. Of particular interest would be the work of Rene Roubicek, Ladislov Oliva, Vera Liskova, the gifted portrait artist Jiri Harcuba, Vaclav Cigler, Pavel Hlava, Ladislav Prenosil, and Ivo Rozsypal.

Scandinavian Tradition of Copper-Wheel Engraving

Another completely different style of design can be found in the pioneering work of Edvard Hald and Simon Gate at Orrefors Glasbruk in Sweden. These two artists represent the first time that nonglass artists were brought into a factory situation on a full-time basis to work in close associa-

tion with the glass workers and engravers. The results created a sensation in the 1920s. Their innovative and sensitive designs established an instant tradition that continues today in Scandinavian crystal design and engraving. Unlike a great deal of work produced during this period, their renderings do not contain the hard-edged angularity of what is often thought of as art deco. Figurative, full of movement, and very sensitive sculpturally, their work represents some of the definitive engraving of that period. Considerable credit must be given to Gustav Abels, the gifted engraver that rendered much of this trend-setting work into crystal. His renderings of fluid dancers, plants, and animals breathe life into the surface of the crystal.

Other Styles of Copper-Wheel Engraving

In addition to the work of the Czech master copper-wheel engravers and the contemporary Scandinavian tradition, there are a number of other styles and individuals who have distinguished themselves in the design and execution of sculpturally sophisticated crystal. The variety of styles of design and the concept of the material illustrated by these various glass artists, gives added insight into the potential of the medium.

The following artists, designers, and companies should be of particular interest: Guido Balsamo-Stella of Venice; Aristide Colette of France; Messrs. Daum of France; Wilhelm Von Eiff, one of the most influential designers and teachers of the twentieth century; Messr. Emile Galle of France; J. & L. Lobmeyr of Austria; Eugene Michel of France; Muller Freres of France; Vicke Lindstrand of Sweden; F. E. Rousseau of France; Joseph Locke of England and later America; Joshua Hodgetts of England; William Fritche of Germany and England; Frederick Carder of England and America, and F. Kretschman of Germany and England.

By studying these and other masterworks of copper-wheel engraving, you should begin to see how the unique properties of transparent sculptural media like glass and crystal are used in creating the illusion of depth and form. It is often surprising to see these works in person, because the amount of space and form suggested in the renderings is generally far greater than you would imagine, considering the amount of material that has been carved away.

A little bit of cutting, skillfully executed, can create a significant illusion of space, form, and movement. This is very important to remember when you design your own carvings and sculptures. Depth of cut is a tool, not an end in itself. Subtlety and restraint will be two of the most difficult characteristics to incorporate into your own designs. Because of the time inherent in executing copper-wheel engraving, this technique of glass decorating has developed with an eye toward saying "more with less." It is a lesson the beginning glass designer should keep in mind in composing original sculptural renderings.

Other Sources

Because the arts of previous cultures generally necessitate a visit to the local library, you might not be inclined to take the time to research these sources. In that case, a very rich source of designs is to be found in your local gift card shop. Many of the larger gift card manufacturers employ highly trained artists who are particularly skilled at graphic design and rendering. That is, they have skill for arranging the elements of a design into a well proportioned and sensitive illustration. These copyrighted designs will all be printed in color, but what you are looking for is the silhouettes of the elements of the design and their arrangement. Remember: enlarge, trace, and simplify. The word *simplify* cannot be overemphasized. In addition to your typical greeting card, look for "embossed" cards. These are cards that have been printed with a sculptured metal die resulting in a bas-relief rendering of the few elements used in making up the design. These cards will often have a single flower or shell on them that will be very suggestive of carved and sculptured glass, particularly if they are printed in a single flower or shell on that will be very suggestive of carved and sculptured glass, particularly if they are printed in a single color. This source of design is very inexpensive, easily accessible, and very broad in subject matter.

SOURCES

Following are a few of the books I have used for years. You should find them to be rich resources of literally hundreds of designs. Keep in mind that the object of using reference materials is not to duplicate the original, but to interpret the design into your own original work. Fortunately this occurs rather naturally because of the different in which the reference designs are rendered and the limitations of sand-carved glass. Before purchasing any of the following books, I suggest you view them at your local library, bookstore, or artist's supply dealer. That way you can determine which ones offer the most potential for your own work. What you want to see in reference artwork is an obvious way of applying the techniques shown in the Comparative Designs in Chapter 3. If you do not see this in a particular item or design, simply go on until you do. With the proper materials, it will not be a long search.

Books

All of these books are suitable for trace-and-use types of art. Many contain camera-ready art and are excellent for photo enlargements or projection with an opaque projector.

Treasury of Chinese Design Motifs (C) 1981
Joseph D'Addetta
Dover Publications, Inc.
180 Varick St.
New York, NY 10014

Early American Cut & Use Stencils (C) 1975
Jo Anne C. Day
Dover Publications, Inc.

Ancient Egyptian Cut and Use Stencils (C) 1978
Theodore Menten
Dover Publications, Inc.

Art Nouveau & Early Art Deco Type & Design (C) 1972
From the Roman Scherer Catalogue
Edited by Theodore Menten
Dover Publications, Inc.

Victorian Stencils for Design and Decoration (C) 1968
Selected by Edmund V. Gillon, Jr.
Dover Publications, Inc.

Art Nouveau, An Anthology of Design and Illustration from The Studio (C) 1969
Selected by Edmund V. Gillon, Jr.
Dover Publications, Inc.

Carouches and Decorative Small Frames, 396 Examples from the Renaissance to Art Deco (C) 1975
Edited by Edmund V. Gillon, Jr.
Dover Publications, Inc.

Art Nouveau Floral Ornament in Color (C) 1976
by M.P. Verneuil et. al.
Edited by Charles Rahn Fry
Dover Publications, Inc.

Art Nouveau Designs in Color (C) 1974
Alphonse Mucha, Maurice Verneuil & Georges Auriol
Dover Publications, Inc.

Japanese Stencil Designs (C) 1967
Andrew W. Tuer
Dover Publications, Inc.

Harter's Picture Archive for Collage and Illustration Over 300 19th Century Cuts (C) 1978
Edited by Jim Harter
Dover Publications, Inc.

The Mucha Poster Coloring Book (C) 1977
Ed Sibbett, Jr.
Dover Publications, Inc.

Art Nouveau Jewelery & Fans (C) 1973
Gabriel Mourey, Aymer Vallance, et. al.
Dover Publications, Inc.

Advertising Art in the Art Deco Style (C) 1975
Selected by Theodore Menten
Dover Publications, Inc.

Pattern Design, An Introduction to the Study of Formal Ornament (C) 1969
Archibald H. Christie
Dover Publications, Inc.

Chinese Folk Designs (C) 1971
A Collection of 300 Cut-Paper Designs
W.M. Hawley
Dover Publications, Inc.

Pattern and Design with Dynamic Symmetry (C) 1967
Edward B. Edwards
Dover Publications, Inc.

Ready-to-Use Floral Designs (C) 1980
Designed by Ed Sibbett, Jr.
Dover Publications, Inc.

A Book of Ornamental Alphabets, Initials, Monograms and Other Designs (C) 1976
Compiled by Universe Books
381 Park Ave. South
New York 10016

A Coloring Book of Japan (C) 1971
Bellerophon Books
36 Anacapa St.
Santa Barbara, CA 93101

The Complete Encyclopedia of Illustration, containing all the Original Illustrations from the 1851 Edition of The Iconographic Encyclopedia of Science, Literature and Art (C) 1979
J.G. Heck
Published by Park Lane
A Division of Crown Publishers
1 Park Ave.
New York 10016

Additional Reference

These books will contain art or items that lend themselves as resource materials for designing sand-carved glass. Others will contain general information on related subjects which would be of interest to the serious student or beginning professional. The titles are very indicative of the materials contained in the books.

Art Nouveau (C) 1969
Renato Barilli
translated by Raymond Rudorff from the Italian original.
The Hamlyn Publishing Group Limited
Hamlyn House
The Centre
Feltham, Middlesex, England

Posters of Mucha (C) 1975
Harmony Books
A Division of Crown Publishers
419 Park Ave. South
New York 10016

The Decorative Thirties (C) 1971
Martin Battersby
Walker and Company
720 5th Ave.
New York 10019

Art Nouveau Posters & Graphics (C) 1977
Roger Stainton
Rizzoli International Publications, Inc.
712 5th Ave.
New York 10019

All Color Book of Art Nouveau (C) 1972
Geoffrey Warren
Distributed in USA by Crescent Books
A Division of Crown Publishers.
Produced by Mandarin Publishers Limited
77A Marble Road
Hong Kong

Audubon's American Birds (C) 1949
Introduction and Notes by Sacheverell Sitwell
B.T. Batsford Ltd.
122 E. 55th St.
New York, NY

The World of Art Deco (C) 1971
Bevis Hillier

Produced and designed by Rainbird Reference Books Limited
Marble Arch House,
44 Edgeware Rd.
London W2.
for the Minneapolis Institute of Arts,
Minneapolis, Minnesota
and E.P. Dutton and Co., Inc.
New York

Cloisonne and Related Arts (C) 1972
W.F. Alexander
Wallace-Homestead Book Company
Des Moines, Iowa

Scandinavian Design, Objects of a Life Style (C) 1975
Eileene Harrison Beer
The American-Scandinavian Foundation
New York

Shells, Treasure from the Sea (C) 1979
James A. Cox
Larousse & Co., Inc.
572 5th Ave.
New York 10036

Animals, A Picture Sourcebook (C) 1979
Edited and Arranged by Don Rice
Van Nostrand Reinhold Company
135 W. 50th St.
New York 10020

How to Draw Animals (C) 1969
Jack Hamm
Grosset & Dunlap
New York

Die Edelstein Gravierkunst
(The Art of Gemstone Engraving)
Ruppenthal-America Ltd., Precious Stones.
576 5th Ave.
New York 10036 (No Copyright)

Manual on Etching Glass (C) 1961
G.M. Heddle
Alec Tiranti Ltd.
72 Charlotte St.
London W1.

Techniques of Gem Cutting, A Lapidary Manual (C)
1966
Herbert Scarfe
Wason-Guptill Publications
1 Astor Plaza
New York 10036

From the Lands of the Scythians, Ancient Treasures from the Museums of the U.S.S.R.
The Metropolitan Museum of Art
New York
Distributed by The New York Graphic Society
(No date of publication or copyright listed.)

The Romance of Seals and Engraved Gems
by Beth B. Sutherland (C) 1965
The Macmillan Company
New York, NY

Glass Books

These books will acquaint you will the work of a broad range of glass artists and their work. Not only do some contain sand-carved glasswork, but familiarity with all aspects of Art Glass is a valuable resource when it comes to designing your own work.

Glass—Art Nouveau to Art Deco (C) 1977
Victor Arwas
Rizzoli Internation Publications, Inc.
712 5th Ave.
New York 10019

English Cameo Glass (C) 1980
Ray and Lee Grover
Crown Publishers
1 Park Ave.
New York 10016
Other publications of particular interest by these

particularly knowledgeable collector/authors are *Art Glass Nouveau, Carved and Decorated European Art Glass,* and *Contemporary Art Glass.*

The Glass of Desire Christian (C) 1978
Jules Traub
The Art Glass Exchange
305 W. Concord Place
Chicago, IL 60614

International Modern Glass (C) 1976
Geoffrey Beard
Charles Scribner's Sons
New York, NY

Ceska, the Art of Glass (C) 1979
CESKA Art Glass
41 Madison Ave.
New York, NY 10021

Czechoslovakian Glass 1350-1980 (C) 1981
A Special Exhibition, The Corning Museum of Glass, Corning, NY
May 2-November 1, 1981
Dover Publications, Inc.

A Selection of Engraved Crystal by Steuben Glass (C) 1961
Steuben Glass
Corning, NY

Complete Cut and Engraved Glass of Corning (C) 1976
E.S. Farrah and J.S. Spillman
Crown Publishers, Inc.
1 Park Ave.
New York, NY 10016

The Glass of Frederick Carder (C)
P.V. Gardner

7

Advanced Projects

These projects are for the student or glass artist wishing to experiment with more challenging techniques in sand carving. Although I can describe the steps involved in obtaining the results you will see, there is no way to communicate how to apply these to all of the designs you may wish to work with. All you can hope to obtain from these projects is an introduction to some of the possibilities of sand carving.

These projects introduce the "secret" of carving and sculpturing, which is the sequential removal of sections of the stencil and the individual carving or sculpturing of each section, one at a time. This is a lengthy process, requiring as much or more time in the planning stage in the actual execution of the decoration. In addition to the time involved, the skill level is significantly greater than other levels of sand carving shown in earlier projects.

The idea in sculpturing glass is to recreate as accurately as possible the spatial relationships of the original image, whether it be reference art or your own creation. Stylization and abstraction are perfectly legitimate and often are necessary with sand carving. The idea is to avoid a spacial faux pas, such as the eye of a subject looking like it is in the middle of the head rather than on the front of the face. If the drawing of a plant suggests that a particular leaf passes in front of another leaf, it is important to maintain this relationship in your glass rendering; otherwise you can end up with a rendering that looks disjointed and bizarre, at best. Levels of your carving will jump around indiscriminately, leaving the impression of disassociation between the individual elements of the design, rather than resulting in a consistent, unified whole. It has been said that the desired effect is one that suggests that the subject was somehow pressed into the glass while it was still molten, resulting in the sculptured effects. While this may not always be the case, it does suggest a beginning goal.

Even though these projects are termed "advanced," they are far from demonstrative of the potential of sand carving, and should be viewed only as introductory illustrations of a few basic principles. The designs were chosen because of their accessibility to the imaginative beginner. The renderings should serve as a starting point for the novice glass sculptor, and not as a collection showing the sculptural potential of this art form.

Through my explanation of the series of steps involved in these projects, I hope you will obtain a feel for how to design and conceive a carving or glass sculpture. That is the most you can hope to obtain. It is impossible to teach the actual sculpturing skills through a book. Only your own direct experience can result in the acquisition of any degree of skill and insight into designing and making your own advanced work.

In addition to working with your own original designs in developing your sand carving skills, I suggest you work with the exercises described in this chapter and perhaps more importantly, look at the designs in the design section of this book and mentally picture a variety of stencil breakdowns for these designs. Try to imagine renderings in Levels 1 through 5 given in Chapter 2 for a number of these designs. In this way you can begin to develop the metal imaging necessary for designing complex glass sculptures.

In working with the projects that follow, remember that you are trying to develop skill in shaping the surface of the glass, not merely blast away as much glass as quickly as possible. For this reasons I suggest you work with pressures between 15 and 30 psi using a 1/8-inch orifice on your blasting nozzle. Any grit size between 100 and 200 should give very satisfactory results. All of these examples were carved with 220-grit silicon carbide at under 20 psi. These lower pressures give you time to shape the glass surface intentionally, rather than merely watching it disappear almost immediately, as happens at higher pressures.

In addition to introducing the sequential removal of stencil material in obtaining carvings and glass sculptures, you will also see the importance of the principle of "deeper cuts first." That is, whatever is deepest cut in a design is the first area to be cut (blasted). This principle is true whether you are working with intaglio or high-relief work. An important difference does exist between these two different types of renderings. In intaglio

work, those areas cut first appear closer to the viewer, once the glass is viewed from the opposite side on which the work was done. In intaglio, deeper cuts appear closer to the viewer. In high-relief work, the opposite is true. Because high-relief work is viewed from the same side from which the work is done, deeper cut areas appear farther away from the viewer. In high-relief work, your deepest cut areas often define the background of the design. See the porcelain plate and the bud vase in the following projects, as examples of this principle.

In working with the sequential removal of the stencil, there is another principle to which you must strictly adhere. That is, you must maintain the edge of all carved/sculptured areas while you are carving all adjacent areas. This edge is the two-dimensional aspect of any design segment or element. This edge may outline a flower petal, for example, while the depth of cut gives the petal form. If you destroy the edge that defines the shape of a segment or section, you have basically destroyed the two-dimensional aspect of that element.

All such edges correspond with the lines in your tracing, which you burnish onto the stencil. All of these lines must be maintained throughout the carving process. In order to do so, you must be aware of exactly where your abrasive blast is hitting the design and the glass. More often than not, when you are carving or sculpturing you will be using only a part of the abrasive blast in order to shape the one section you are working on. You must then be conscious of where the remainder of the blast is going. You must expose already blasted areas as little as possible; otherwise, destruction or distortion of a design element will result.

This concept may be difficult to grasp until you are actually working on a glass design and become aware of the destructive power of even the slight edge of the abrasive blast. Low blasting pressures and small nozzle orifices will give you flexibility for virtually any design.

EXERCISES FOR
THE NOVICE GLASS SCULPTOR

In addition to working with actual designs in your experiments with sand carving, it is also very useful to practice carving or sculpturing preconceived forms into the glass based on simple geometric shapes cut out of the stencil. In other words, cut small geometric shapes, such as squares, rectangles, ovals, and circles, into the stencil covering small pieces of scrap plate glass 1/2 or 3/4 inch in thickness. (These cut offs are often available from local flat glass dealers.) Remove the stencil from the glass, exposing a single shape at a time, then sculpt the shape into the form you imagined before you began your blasting. The shaping of these simple shapes into forms is accomplished by varying the movement of your blasting nozzle. (See Fig. 7-1.)

As an example, your first shape may be a 3- x -6-inch rectangle. Remove this section of sten-

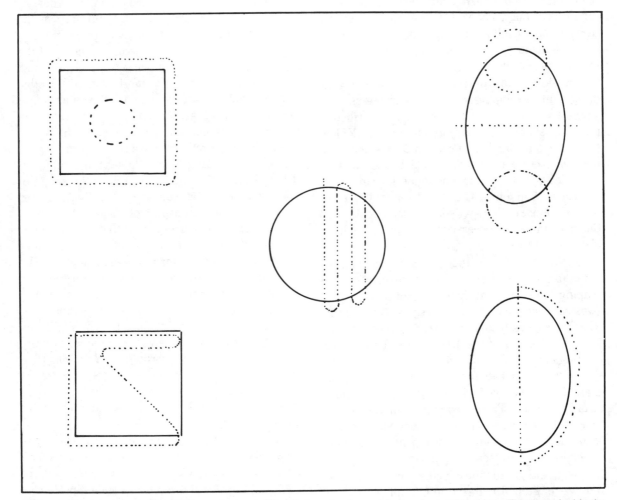

Fig. 7-1. Line drawings of several suggested exercises for learning to sculpt glass by sand carving. The areas inside the solid lines are exposed to the sand blast, while those areas outside the solid border are masked with stencil. The dotted lines indicate the path of the blasting nozzle over the exposed glass. When you are blasting such patterns it is important not only to vary the patterns per se (work with circles, squares, rectangles, ovals, triangles, etc.), but to vary the distance between the glass and the blasting nozzle while you are moving through the pattern. In other words, at one point in the pattern you may be 2 inches from the glass, and in another part of the pattern you may be 6 inches from the glass. You should also vary the angle of the nozzle to the glass so you are not always blasting at a 90-degree angle. In this way you will be able to obtain an infinite variety of forms from very simple shapes cut into the stencil. With a little practice, the variety of effects you can obtain will surprise you.

cil, exposing the rectangle to the abrasive blast. Then by varying the blasting distance and the pattern of movement of your blasting nozzle in relation to the exposed glass, you can create an almost unlimited number of forms. Your rectangle may be rounded in the center and taper out to both ends; it may be cut very deep at one end, creating an angle, then change into a full roundness in the center, and be relatively shallow at the other end; it may be peaked out at each corner and very shallow in the center, etc.

The object of this exercise is two-fold. First you must get into the habit of first visualizing exactly what it is you wish to achieve in your sculptured form. Secondly you must practice obtaining that precise form.

This exercise will help you become aware of some of the limitations of sand carving, but more importantly, it will open your eyes to alternatives that you didn't know were possible.

This type of exercise is also helpful in developing a necessary mental skill you must have before you can consistently and predictably obtain artistic results in your sculptured work. This skill involves being able to see the desired form in reverse. When most people conceive of a sculptured form, it is generally seen in the mind's eye as being viewed from the front angle; i.e., when you think of a rose, you are seeing the rose from the front. In carving and sculpturing glass, you must also be able to conceive of this form in reverse. You must be able to see how this form can be cut into a flat surface on one side of the glass so that the desired sculptured form is seen from the other side. While this may sound confusing, and it is sometimes, it is, for the most part, a mechanical skill that is acquired with practice.

A good way to conceive of this image reversal is to think of your form as being inflated from the back side. This is what is actually happening during the sand carving process. You are forcing air and abrasive at the glass surface, inflating your design into the surface of the glass.

This image reversal is where many would-be glass sculptors get lost in a haze of confusion and do not realize what is necessary. They begin with

an excellent concept of the desired form, work out the stencil breakdown, get everything ready, and once in the blasting booth are faced with a design that has a reversed left-to-right orientation than their original rendering, and must be sculpted in reverse to the picture in their mind. That is why you should anticipate the need for practice and a learning period in which you go through a lot a mental exercise. Viewing examples of repousse metal work from both sides is often helpful, as is working with repousse, if it is convenient. During this period of learning, you will also understand why more time is generally spend conceiving and planning a sculptured design, than in actually carrying out the glass work.

Finally, I will pass on the best piece of advice I was ever given with respect to sand carving. During a discussion with Mr. Ivan Pogue, one of the premier American glass sculptors working over the past 40 years, he advised me to "be patient." That single admonition will serve the dedicated student of sand carving better than any other.

FLORAL MOTIF ON FLAT GLASS

In this project you will take one of the suggested design sources mentioned in Chapter 6 and

Fig. 7-2. The front of the locket.

graphically illustrate how to use it to fabricate your own design. In this case an inexpensive Victorian locket was purchased at a flea market for less than $1.00 and taken to a typesetting house where enlargements were made on paper (sometimes called *stats, photostats*, or *paper positives*). (See Figs. 7-2 and 7-3.) I then used white acrylic paint to "white out" all of the design that interfered with the tracing of the desired parts of the design (see Fig. 7-4). Afterward I placed a piece of tracing paper over the stat, and, referring to my original locket, made a pencil tracing of those parts of the design I wanted in our glass carving. It is important to have your enlargement made to exactly the size you want your design on the glass. In this way your tracing is ready to burnish and use once it is completed. Because of the very high degree of modeling and form given to the original design on the locket, it is an excellent piece of reference art on which to base sculptured glass. It may be helpful for you to keep the original handy during the actual sculpturing process so that you can refer to it if there is any confusion about the placement or shaping of any sections.

This design was sculptured into 1/2-inch plate glass using all of the preparation steps outlined in the first flat glass project in Chapter 4.

As with all carved or sculptured glass designs, you must first divide the motif into discrete sections that must be internally consistent, and then determine a carving order that results in the desired spacial relationship. In this particular example, I had the original locket to refer to for placement and form.

I labeled my sections as follows: blossoms A, B; other sculptured sections 12, 13, 14, 15; leaves 16 through 21; and stems 22 through 27 (Fig. 7-5). Thus, even though it appears to be a complex design with many different levels, it actually only has four basic sections that need to be internally consistent and relate to each other. I then needed to look at each section and determine an order for carving each segment of it in order to give me the sculptural look. Referring to my original locket and beginning with the blossoms, I decided which parts should be deeper than other segments, and I

numbered the segments in order (1-11). This same sequence was followed for each blossom. Sections 12 through 15 were made up of only one stencil segment each; thus, all shaping of these segments was solely dependent on the action of the blasting nozzle. I then determined the sequence necessary for the leaves which would give the desired look. The last section was the stems which are scattered all over the design. All I had to do was allow for the forward placement of all the other elements of the design in relation to the stems, and make sure that stem #22 passed in front of stem #23, and the sequence was determined.

Remember deeper cuts first in determining your sequences, both within the design sections and in determining which sections are carved before others. This simple rule, consistently applied, will form the basis for determining the sequencing of all of your carved and sculptured work.

The final sequence for this design was as follows: Blossom A, sections 1 through 11, then Blossom B in the same sequence, then sections 12 through 15. I proceeded to the leaves, following the numbers 16 through 21. The stems were last, sections 22 through 27 in order. This sequence resulted in the design as shown in Figs. 7-6 and 7-7.

If you look at the finished sculptured design, you should realize that much of the appearance of this design depends on the shaping of a number of the segments and not the mechanical blasting of a predetermined sequence. Look at sections 12 through 15 in particular. Each of these areas is made up of one section only, yet a distinct form must be given to each in order to communicate the character of the section within the overall design. While it would be possible to mechanically blast each of these sections to obtain a sort of flat deep-cut and still have an attractive design, the object of this project is to begin to shape the surface of the glass in each section in a way that adds to the sculptural look. Of all the sections in this design, 12 through 15 are by far the most difficult to shape.

Look closely at section 13. Note how the upper portion is full and round, with the depth of cut then decreasing as you move to the bottom of the motif. Then along the bottom edge the depth again in-

Fig. 7-3. Unretouched stat enlargement of the locket.

Fig. 7-4. The original stat, having been retouched with white acrylic paint. All of the background has been covered in order to make tracing of the dominant features of the design easier.

Fig. 7-5. The finished tracing of the retouched locket photostat (Fig. 7-4), with the sections numbered in order for sculpturing.

Fig. 7-6. The finished sculptured design from Fig. 7-5. The overall size of the design is 5 × 6 inches.

creases to the point of creating a peaked-out edge cut into the glass running along the bottom. Note how the shaping is even and consistent, moving evenly from deep to shallow sections, without "nozzle trails." Also note how there is no obtrusive edge on the upper portion of the motif. This means that the depth of cut tapers evenly from the edge into the center deepest area. Section 15 is another example of a well-shaped section that requires control.

In looking at Fig. 7-6, be sure to note how certain sections seem to pass in front of other sections. Look at section 12 and the tops of sections 16 through 18. Look at sections 22 and 23 in relation to section 12. Look at the intersection of sections 22 and 23. Sequencing results in this appearance. Remember, if it is deeper, it was cut first. By

remembering this rule, you should, in time, be able to look at a glass carving or sculpture and be able to determine the sequence in which the work was done.

HIGH-RELIEF BUD VASE

In this project, an antique bud vase slightly less than 6 inches tall will be sand-carved in a sculptured, high-relief iris motif traced from an art nouveau design book. This project is important because it demonstrates how to work in high-relief and on an irregularly shaped item, and how to avoid having to draw free hand (as is often necessary when you are carving vases) on the stencil material after you have applied it to the item being decorated. This particular vase is another example of an item purchased for a fraction of its retail replacement value. It was purchased for less than $1.00 from an antique dealer.

Because most of the preparation steps in this project have not been shown in the beginning-level projects, I have shown this project in a step-by-step series of photographs (Figs. 7-8 through 7-14). Additionally, I have then shown two different intaglio interpretations of the same iris design. Thus, you can see one design done in high-relief and intaglio, with the necessary sequence of stencil removal outlined.

Just as with the previous advanced projects, the first step after you have a tracing of your design is to break it down into some number of sections that reflect the major areas making up the design (Fig. 7-15). In this case, there is the background, the leaves/stem, and the flower or petals. You must include the background because this is a high-relief

rendering, and the background must be cut back, establishing the relief of the actual flower motif. Also subdivide the flower petals into primary areas (those that are closest to the viewer) and secondary areas (those that are carved back slightly, giving two levels to each petal).

First of all, carve the background, labeled #1 in Fig. 7-15. The deeper you blast, the higher the flower motif will stand off the background, and the more glass you will have available for shaping during the actual sculpturing of the flower petals. After this step is accomplished, proceed to the leaves/ stem area. Blast these in order as numbered 2 through 5. Note how this sequence places the leaves in relation to each other and the stem. Look at which parts are made to look like they pass in front of other parts.

Then proceed to the actual flower. Because each petal of the flower is broken down into two

Fig. 7-7. Closeup of Fig. 7-6.

145

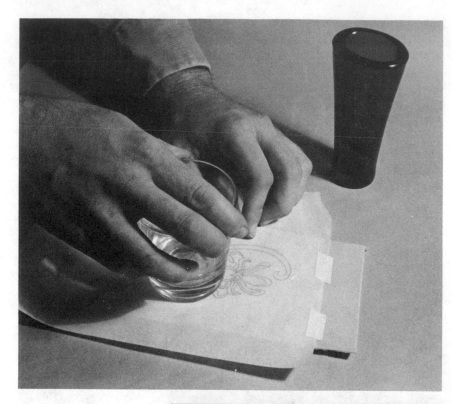

Fig. 7-8. The tracing of Fig. 7-15 is burnished onto the stencil prior to placement on the vase.

Fig. 7-9. Another view of Fig. 7-8.

Fig. 7-10. After burnishing the stencil is trimmed for easy handling prior to placement on the vase.

parts, you must make one part appear closer to the viewer than the other part. I chose to cut the "center" part of each petal back, giving the "outside" of each pedal precedence. Then carve back each section as labeled, 6 though 13. You are now ready to carve the last stage of this rendering.

The areas you will work on next are those that will be closest to the viewer and will require the least amount of blasting. These areas also offer the most opportunity for sculptural shaping, due to their height off the background and their function within the design. If these areas were merely frosted or etched after cutting all the other areas back as shown, you would still have an attractive piece, but it would not show much of the sculptural potential of this design. The primary areas of the petals would have the flat appearance of the stem and leaves.

In carving the primary sections, proceed as numbered, 14 through 21. Those areas that allowed for the most shaping of the glass surface are 14, 15, and 21 because of their size and function within the design.

The last area to be blasted is the center sections, 22 and 23. The finished design is shown in

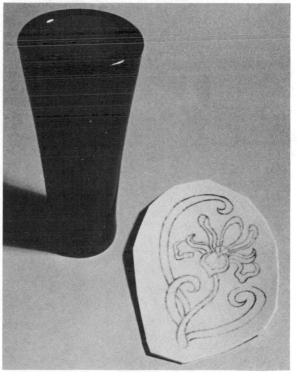

Fig. 7-11. The tracing of Fig. 7-15 is burnished onto the stencil prior to placement on the vase.

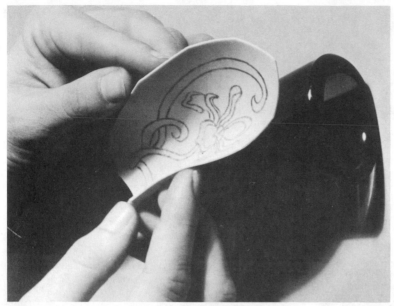

Fig. 7-12. Another view of Fig. 7-8.

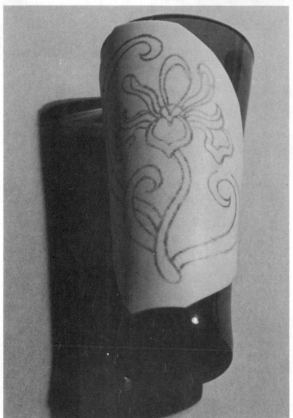

Fig. 7-13. After burnishing the stencil is trimmed for easy handling prior to placement on the vase.

Fig. 7-14. The tracing of Fig. 7-15 is burnished onto the stencil prior to placement on the vase.

Fig. 7-15. This is the design that was burnished on the vase in Fig. 7-8.

Fig. 7-16. Following the sequence described, this is the completed vase. After carving, I took this piece to a local art glass studio and had it acid-polished to a more translucent finish. Note that the entire surface of the vase has been etched after sculpturing.

Figs. 7-16 and 7-17. For the intaglio renderings, we have renumbered the order in which the elements of the design are carved. Because this is an intaglio rendering on flat glass, there is no background to carve back; thus, that step is eliminated. Simply follow the numbers 1 through 22 in Fig. 7-18.

If you look closely at the two renderings, you should be able to see the difference between them (Figs. 7-19 and 7-20). Look at the areas I previously called secondary petals and leaves 20 and 21, as numbered in the intaglio sequence. In Intaglio #1, I deep-cut the primary petals and simply etched the secondary petals, resulting in a somewhat flat appearance to those areas. Also deep-cut are the petals, 20 and 21 individually, thus placing 20 "on top of" 21.

In Intaglio #2, I deep-cut and added some de-

gree of form to the secondary petals (note the fullness and highlights on the edges) and cut leaves 20 and 21 at the same time, thus running them together where they intersect. This graphically demonstrates the difference between sequentially carving overlapping areas and carving them at the same time. While the degree of form imparted to each leaf is approximately the same, the suggestion of overlapping is far greater in Intaglio #1 due to this sequencing.

SCULPTURED PORCELAIN PLATE

In this project, an inexpensive porcelain plate is sculptured with a fish motif in high-relief. Both the subject of the design—the fish—and the background are sculptured, suggesting both form and movement.

Fig. 7-17. Close-up of the completed vase.

Fig. 7-18. Stencil breakdown and sequence numbering for intaglio renderings #1 and #2 shown in Figs. 7-19 and 7-20.

Fig. 7-19. Intaglio #1. Note the flat secondary areas (the centers of the petals). Note, too, the relative positions of the leaves to each other and the stem. Compare with Fig. 7-20.

All the preparatory steps for this project were identical to the beginning-level porcelain project. For that reason those steps will not be repeated here. Because this type of work is the result of following a particular sequence during the carving process combined with some degree of skill of the artisan doing the work, I can only describe the sequence followed in this particular design and cannot precisely describe how a novice can obtain the results you see. (See Fig. 7-22.)

To begin with, I carved the background first because of the general rule in sand carving that deeper cuts first. There are exceptions, but these become too complex for this outline, and are generally discovered in practice. Beginning at the bottom (although I could have started at the top), I carved sections 1 through 9 in order. This places the fish "on top" of the wave patterns.

I then began working on the fish at the tail. Because I wanted the center section of the tail to be closest to the viewer I cut the sections of the tail in order, as numbered 10 through 14. I then carved the dorsal fin to put the end of the fins that intersect with the body under the scales. It would look awkward to have fins looking like appliques laying on top of the scales. These were carved in order, 15 through 17.

I then progressed to the top fin for the same

Fig. 7-20. Intaglio #2. Note how the secondary areas have a fullness to them. Note also how the leaves on the right side that intersect are run together. Compare with the same area on Fig. 7-19.

Fig. 7-21. Line drawing of the fish motif as burnished onto the stencil.   Numbers indicate the order in which each section was carved. The overall design is 6 inches in diameter.

reason. This section was carved in order, 18 through 23. Then I went back to the tail and began with the scales of the body, carving them in order as numbered, 24 through 52.

The next step is the head. The deepest sections on the head are the center of the eye and mouth and the small section which would be the "chin." These sections, 53 through 55, were carved first.

Then I proceeded with the head and carved sections 56 through 61. The result was that the mouth has preeminence over immediately adjacent parts and the top section (57) of the head (the area surrounding the eye) has a similar relationship to the "jaw" area.

As you can see, this design was broken down into sections (background, tail, dorsal fin, top fin,

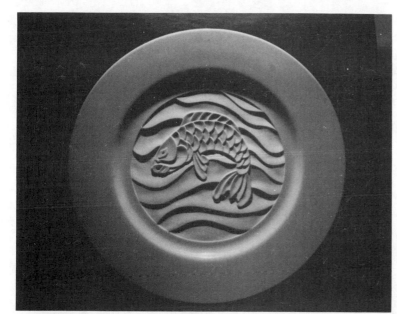

Fig. 7-22. The completed plate.

Fig. 7-23. Close-up of the sculptured design.

body, head), then a sequence was determined for each section. You should not approach any design by trying to determine the entire sequence at one time. Begin by first breaking the design into obvious sections that must be carved so they are internally consistent. Then determine how each section must relate to those sections immediately adjacent to it. Don't worry how the tail relates to the head, or the body to the mouth. Think only of immediately adjacent areas. Once you have determined the sections of your design and know how you want those sections to relate to each other, you should have no problem determining which section should be "in front" of which. Then apply the rule, deeper cuts first and determine your carving sequence. See Figs. 7-22 and 7-23.

Alternative Techniques

8

In addition to the more traditional sand carving techniques involving hand-cut stencils, die-cut stencils, and nonadhesive templates, there are other techniques used in protecting those areas of the glass that are not to be etched. Additionally, there are a number of other, totally different processes that are used in obtaining etched, engraved, or sculptured renderings on glass and crystal. Although all of these processes may not be of interest to the hobbyist or glass artist, it is good to have a basic knowledge of these alternatives if you ever consider buying glass decoration services or if you run across them in your gift buying.

Each of these alternatives will vary greatly with respect to the final appearance of the decoration, the equipment necessary to complete the work, the quantities that are most appropriate for each technique, and the skill necessary to design and execute the work. Some are purely mechanical in their reproduction of the design, while others are the result of years, if not decades, of artistic training. The price range of the items decorated or manufactured through these processes will vary from less than one dollar retail to tens of thousands of dollars for the most skillful and artistic techniques.

In reviewing these alternatives, it is important to remember that one is not better than another. Each has its own physical characteristics and applications which makes it appropriate for specific glass decorating situations. The buyer of decorated glass should be informed of these techniques so that intelligent decisions can be made concerning which is best suited for the quantity, quality, and price range needed.

SCREEN-PRINTED RESISTS

This process, probably more than any other used in association with sand blasting, has been reinvented by more people in more places than virtually any other technique in current use. The reason is that screen printing can be done with extreme speed and precision, using both manual and automatic equipment. Screen printing is very straightforward and apparently very easy to do; thus, it is very attractive to the person interested in duplications, detail, and efficiency.

As applied to sand carving, the results are often less than expected, particularly in relation to depth of cut and good clean lines between etched areas and clear areas. The depth of cut generally obtained through the use of screen-applied resists would be best described as surface etching, although more advanced processes are capable of obtaining some degree of depth of cut that might border on what I would call engraving. The "saw-toothed" edge inherent in printing high-viscosity materials like the most common screen-printed resists limits its application where the finest quality decoration is required.

As currently practiced, it involves the screening of plastisol-based materials (used more commonly for screening onto fabrics like T-shirts or handbags) onto the surface of the glass, curing this plastisol in ovens for 4 to 6 minutes in order to harden the resist, then blasting. A particular variation of this process was patented by Owens-Illinois Glass Company in the mid 1960s that is probably the definitive technique with regards to screen-printed resists. Copies of this patent are available from the U.S. Patent Office for a nominal sum, and would be of interest to anyone wishing to avoid reinventing the wheel.

The most common use of this decorating technique involves decorating duplicate flat glass panels with detailed etched designs for commercial architectural installations. For these installations, it is very cost efficient and offers a lot of "look" on the glass for what is generally a very reasonable price. Architects and interior designers should find this technique very useful in incorporating extremely detailed etched glass designs into their projects.

IMPELLER BLASTING

This process is not sand carving in the traditional sense at all. It requires no compressor, no sand-blast generator, no nozzles, and no separate blasting room or cabinet. In this technique, a very fast moving blade or propeller (the impeller) agitates the abrasive grit within the very small confines of an etching chamber to such a velocity that surface etching occurs as the abrasive grit strikes the glass.

Traditional templates are used to protect those areas that are not to be etched. These units are very compact, usually less than the size of a loaf of bread, and are best used for surface etching glassware, ashtrays, and the like. Used for years in cleaning spark plugs, this compact and efficient etching setup is now used in the glassware trade.

The greatest application would seem to be with glass retailers or small studios offering custom etching on moderate quantities of glassware and other small decorative accessories. Larger quantities would best be decorated with semiautomatic or fully automatic equipment.

For the buyer interested in custom-decorated items, where the quantity is not sufficient for the larger commercial glassware decorating companies, this technique should offer an alternative. By calling glass retailers listed in your Yellow Pages under "Gift Shops" or "Crystal," you should be able to determine if this service is available in your area.

PRESSED OR MOLDED GLASS

This is a manufacturing technique utilized when the glass is in a molten state and the glass article is being fabricated. Using a preformed mold, the molten glass is pressed into the desired shape, including all necessary decoration. This technique is similar to that used by notary publics in embossing legal documents, although the glass objects manufactured with this technique are very sculptural, and are often figurative.

A variation of this technique is *mold blown*, in which the glass is blown (by mouth or utilizing compressed air) into a mold in order to obtain the predetermined design on the outside surface of a vase, bowl, or glassware item. Where pressing would usually refer to a solid piece of glass, a blown piece is most often hollow or in the shape of a utilitarian vessel. Often, the molded decoration or sculptural form is not etched (not given a white, frosty appearance) and remains clear. Virtually all of the production of the Cristal Lalique factory in France is produced using one of these two variations of molded glass.

Because of the expense of the fabrication of the multipiece mold necessary for this manufacturing process and the sophisticated fabrication facilities, this is not a technique that the typical glass hobbyist or glass artist can perform. Buyers interested in this technique should understand that until quantities approaching 10,000 to 20,000 pieces are required, it tends to be prohibitively expensive. Delivery times of 6 to 12 months are common when special-ordering this type of work.

WHEEL CUTTING

I will include copper-wheel engraving, stone-wheel cutting, and diamond-wheel cutting in this description. This is one of the most common forms of hand-applied decoration on glassware and other accessories such as bowls and vases. While *cutting* generally refers to simple floral motifs, precisely cut geometric patterns, or facetlike cuts, *engraving* is usually reserved for reference to more sensitive renderings of figures, animals, and complete scenes.

This type of decoration involves the use of grinding wheels, attached to a rotating spindle, to incise the surface of the glass. Its foundation lies with gemstone engraving and cutting, and is often virtually identical to lapidary techniques.

Copper wheels tend to be rather small in relation to traditional stone cutting wheels. They obtain their cutting action on the glass by being "charged" with Carborundum and light oil or water. Stone wheels are generally made of Carborundum or aluminum oxide grits bonded together with baked resins. They will vary greatly in size and may be several feet in diameter. Constant *trueing*, or shaping and resurfacing, is required in order to maintain the desired shape and cutting action of these wheels.

Diamond wheels are made of metal alloys that are permanently impregnated with diamond dust. They also require resurfacing in order to maintain the desired cutting action.

The depth of cut found in wheel cut decorations will vary considerably and will range from very shallow cuts to very deep and sculptural renderings. A considerable amount of training and acquired skill are necessary to successfully execute high-quality wheel cutting or engraving. Most people

skilled in this art have gone through years of training in order to execute quality work. It has been said that a master engraver does not reach his artistic prime until after the age of 60, having perhaps been apprenticed at the age of 15. The work of the Czechoslovakian engravers over the past 300 years best exemplifies the potential of this technique. Their technical and artistic dominance in this field is well recognized throughout the world.

Wheel cutting is an excellent way of applying simple floral motifs and monograms to large quantities of glass items, and for executing the finest-quality sculptural engravings within a certain size range. The size typical of most sand-carved glass work would be considered very large in relation to most wheel-cut engravings. Although it may be impractical for larger pieces of glass, wheel engraving is the finest and most versatile technique for expressing the artistic potential of sculpturally decorated glass because of its near infinite control in the hands of a skilled master engraver.

Because of the number of wheels necessary to execute what appear to be relatively simple designs, and the training required to produce high-quality work, this is not a technique that can easily be done by the hobbyist or artisan as can sand carving.

DIAMOND-POINT ENGRAVING

Developed in the eighteenth century by a few Dutchmen, several of whom were English extraction, this technique involves the pricking, drawing, and stippling of the design onto the glass surface with a diamond-tipped "pencil" or steel-carbide tool. The work is generally done completely freehand, although some artists use a variety of techniques to add to the visibility of the design in progress or to add important guidelines prior to beginning the engraving. Like copper-wheel engraving, it is a very time-consuming and unforgiving process, dependent completely on the artistic ability of the engraver. No templates, stencils, or similar devices are available to the diamond-point artist.

By varying the material the point is made of, whether carbide steel or diamonds in various states of sharpness, and the pressure and angle of application to the glass, a remarkable variation in tone, line, and texture can be achieved by the skilled engraver. Considering this technique is not capable of what would be termed deep cutting compared to copper-wheel cutting or sand carving, the degree of form that can be suggested is truly remarkable. Portraiture, architectural renderings, and coats of arms are three of the most common types of designs rendered using this technique.

Generally reserved for one-of-a-kind art pieces, this technique is not widely used by glass decorators. Most often the finest full lead crystal stems are engraved for important presentation pieces or commemoratives. Those glass artists who specialize in this engraving technique are virtually always self-taught and have spent many years perfecting and refining their skills. Most of their work is accepted on a commission basis, just as with any other type of unique artwork. The number of state-of-the-art diamond-point engravers working today could probably be counted on one hand, and most reside in Great Britain where this technique is currently undergoing a revival of interest.

For those interested in seeing more of this very rare glass engraving technique, I suggest you review the work of Franz Greenwood and David Wolff, both of whom worked in Holland in the eighteenth century. Contemporary exponents include W.J. Wilson, D.B. Peace, Lawrence Whistler, H. Warren Wilson, and William Meadows, all of Great Britain. The work of the Swiss artist Gertrude Bohnert would also be of interest.

See Figs. 8-1 through 8-3 for examples of the work of William Meadows. His work illustrates the degree of form and subtlety that can be achieved using this technique of glass engraving.

ACID ETCHING

Today this technique is most often used for lightly etching designs onto mass-produced glassware or lighting fixtures. These designs are usually floral or simply decorative in nature and do not exhibit any degree of form inherent in other types of incised or engraved glass.

At the turn of the century and earlier, it was a very common technique utilized for a wide range

Fig. 8-1. Diamond-point engraving of the "Cothay" family home of The Right Honorable Edward du Cann, M.P. in Somerset, England. Note the superb suggestion of form in the stonework of the house, and the shading in the front lawn and clouds. Engraving by Mr. William Meadows.

of applications. It was used for decorating large quantities of glassware, vases, bowls, and lighting fixtures; roughing out cameo glass prior to carving; and etching large architectural panels.

In addition to being used to cut into and decorate glass, acid etching has often been used to impart various surface textures to the glass. This procedure is accomplished by varying the constituents of the glass batch and the precise measurements of the chemicals mixed with

Fig. 8-2. Full lead crystal goblet representing one of a series depicting the flowers of each season. This one is "Summer; Rose and Honeysuckle." It is important to remember, that in diamond-point engraving every dot is added one at a time. The result is that the design is "built up" little by little—a very lengthy and painstaking process. Engraving by Mr. William Meadows.

hydrofluoric acid (which actually eats into the glass). Sand carving and grit etching have now replaced a number of applications of acid etching, including roughing out cameo glass and decorating large architectural panels.

Acid etching tends to be characterized by a slightly rougher edge between clear areas and etched areas than is obtainable with grit etching. It does not afford the control of depth and shaping inherent in sand carving. In most cases, it will also not exhibit quite the degree of "whiteness" in the decoration as is evident in sand carving. See "French Embossing" in the Glossary for more information.

In addition to acid etching, hydrofluoric-acid-based chemicals can be used to polish glass, particularly lead crystal and full lead crystal. In this procedure, mild acid solutions are used to impart a final, brilliant polish to wheel-cut designs, particularly facetlike cuts. The entire article is immersed in an acid bath for repeated short term dips lasting from 10 to 30 seconds, until the desired polish is obtained. Most cut glass receives its final polish this way.

Because of the danger in dealing with powerful hydrofluoric acid solutions, this technique is not practical for small-to-moderate-sized glass decorators. Hobbyists and artisans can obtain most effects similar to acid work through sand carving.

The buyer of decoration services is finding that acid etched pieces are becoming more difficult to obtain as sand carving becomes more widespread. Acid-etched architectural panels and lighting fixtures would be the easiest articles to obtain on a custom basis. Acid-etched mirrors and glassware may still be obtained from a very select number of decorators, although cost factors and flexibility with respect to the final rendering on the glass may make sand carving the technique of choice.

ACID CREAM

This technique involves the use of solutions containing hydrofluoric acid mixed with a carrier compound which results in a thick, creamy consistency. After masking the glass in a manner similar to hand-cut or die-cut stencils, this cream can be applied to the exposed portions of the glass. After approximately 1 minute of exposure, the cream is washed off with warm water. The result is a matte-white frosted surface where the cream was applied.

For someone who wants to obtain a permanent white decoration on glass and finds it impossible to gain access to sand carving equipment, this offers an accessible alternative. Although you will not obtain any depth of cut whatsoever, you will have a permanent, white, etched design. It will have the appearance of very light sand blasting using a very, very fine grit. It is useless for cutting through flashed glass, roughing out cameo glass, or any other application where depth of cut is required.

One of the primary advantages is that this cream can be screen-printed directly onto the glass; thus, production of multiples is accessible to the hobbyist or glass artisan who wants to make inexpensive surface etchings with a minimum of equipment. If you are interested in screen-printed resists for sand carving, you should investigate this alternative before you invest too much time or money in developing the fine points required for satisfactory results using plastisol-based resists.

Because these creams utilize hydrofluoric-acid-based chemicals, you should follow all the standard precautions involved in using corrosive solutions. Good ventilation and protection for your eyes and skin is required. Sources are listed in the Appendix. See also *acid badging* in the Glossary.

ULTRASONIC ENGRAVING

This technique is one of the more curious techniques that is in current use in the glass decorating industry. It works on the principle of changing ultrasonic sound to linear (back and forth) motion, which is used to vibrate a metal die, cut in the form of the desired decoration. An abrasive slurry, such as Carborundum and water, is flushed between the vibrating die and the glass or crystal, providing the cutting action. These decorations tend to be very sculptural in nature and very deep-cut. Most items decorated by this technique are paperweights, crystal blocks, and necklace pendants.

Because of the complex setup procedures in fabricating the original dies and the fact that the

Fig. 8-3. Full lead crystal goblet that has been diamond-point engraved with the family coat of arms of the Downing family of England. Note the shading on the central figure and the lettering left clear in the banner at the bottom of the design. These characteristics are particularly difficult to obtain. Engraving by Mr. William Meadows.

die is also eaten away by the abrasive slurry, this technique is not widely used. Considering that a production ultrasonic engraving machine can cost from $30,000 to $60,000 and up, you can see why many decorators do not offer this type of service.

The most common application of the ultrasonic technology is in the drilling of gemstone beads for necklaces and in machining so-called space-age metals, which cannot be machined by any other means. This technique is so precise that it is used to carve what appears to be a very fine wire mesh screen out of a solid plate of metal.

For engraving glass articles, it exhibits an interesting effect, in that the design can be cut to any depth in the glass, and the rendering of the design will remain the same. In other words, distortion does not develop as depth increases, which is in contrast to both sand carving and acid etching.

Examples of ultrasonic work can be seen at a number of finer gift and card shops that offer full lead crystal with sculptured designs. The finest quality crystal engraving blocks and necklace pendants are available from these outlets. This technique has also been used in manufacturing beautifully sculptured limited-edition paperweights marketed nationally through collector mints and societies.

Some crystal aficionados may discount this decorating technique as too mechanical to be worthy of purchase, but this attitude is very unfair, considering the quality of material that is generally decorated and the very well conceived sculptural renderings that are common to this very advanced technical process. When you consider that this technique can approach the subtlety of fine copper-wheel engraving for a fraction of the cost, and that most times are produced in limited quantities, these items could easily become collector's items in the future. As with all glass decorating, its value should be based on the quality of the article that is decorated, the concept of the design, and its appropriateness for glass, rather than based solely on the decorating technique.

This technique is useful when thousands of blanks are to be fabricated and decorated with a number of designs, the quantities of which may not reach the minimum necessary to make pressing practical. If the quality of the rendering must be superior to what is available through pressing, ultrasonic engraving may also be the technique of choice, even though pressing is practical. Items with curved surfaces and made from anything less than fine lead crystal are generally impossible or unworthy of decoration using ultrasonic techniques.

LASER ETCHING

Very recently techniques have come onto the market which are based on laser technology. Working from camera-ready black-and-white art, these techniques are used to duplicate very detailed designs, such as letter styles, corporate logos, college emblems, and other detailed designs that require extremely accurate, detailed duplication.

These techniques have been used to decorate glassware and a number of crystal paperweights and pendant-sized items. Because of the degree of mechanization in these processes, coupled with minimal setup procedures, these high-tech processes are very cost efficient in relation to other etching processes. Unlike photo-process sand carving, which also is used in duplicating extremely detailed designs, laser techniques result only in a surface etching, with none of the light-catching characteristics inherent in deep-cut engraved crystal or glass.

A variation on laser cutting that is practiced in Europe is the use of a computer-guided laser to cut through an acid resist. The prepared item is then exposed to hydrofluoric acid, resulting in an exceptionally detailed acid etch. This process is also used on paperweights and necklace pendants, with decoration services available through factory representatives. So far the biggest market for these processes is in the advertising specialties market and selected consumer items. Large-scale decorating of flat glass, mirrors, or other non-lead crystal articles is not currently available.

If you are interested in obtaining more information on these processes, you should keep abreast of patent applications. It is anticipated that a patent or patents covering these techniques may be granted in the near future.

Appendix

Sources

This Appendix lists sources for all the materials mentioned in this book. It is important to note that many of these suppliers cater to a specific market (hobbyists, artists, trade professionals); thus, not all suppliers may sell in quantities consistent with your needs. I have therefore listed a number of sources for all materials. It is important to try and contact the supplier who generally supplies materials to persons like yourself. Fortunately, supplies for all necessary materials are easily within reach to anyone that makes the effort to obtain them, whether you need stencil material and flat glass by the mile or by the square foot.

In addition to the companies listed, many others are listed in *Glass Studio*, a magazine dedicated to stained glass and other art glass specialties. If you are a professional stained glass artist, or have a studio, you should be able to purchase materials directly from the many wholesale suppliers that advertise in this magazine. If you are a student or hobbyist, you should anticipate purchasing most of their stained glass related materials from retail suppliers in your area. *Glass Studio* is available from

many stained glass retailers, with subscriptions available from the publisher by writing:

Glass Studio Magazine
P.O. Box 23383
Portland, OR 97223

MATERIALS TO BE DECORATED

Glassware, Plates, Bowls. Retail outlets such as gift/card shops, large department stores, grocery stores, and glass factory outlets will offer a wide variety of glass items suitable for sand carving and engraving. Watch for sales, particularly on inexpensive lead crystal and domestically made crystal glass articles. Garage sales, flea markets, estate sales, and antique dealers are excellent sources for unique items such as the vase and decanter shown in this book.

If you are interested in large wholesale quantities for production work, you must contact manufacturers directly or through their sales agents.

Flat Glass. 1/4-, 3/8-, 1/2-, and 3/4-inch clear float plate glass, and grey, bronze, peach, blue, and gold float plate glass, sometimes available as mirrors. Stock sizes of thick tabletops, and custom orders for special cut sizes and edge work. Retail flat glass dealers listed in your Yellow Pages under "Glass" should be able to tell you of the availability of these materials in your area. Always try several dealers for pricing and availability of stock materials. If you are interested in large wholesale quantities for production work, you must contact manufacturers directly.

Stained Glass. Such materials as flashed glass, small beveled shapes (sometimes in colors or mirrors), dalles, rondels, etc. Check your Yellow Pages for local retail dealers listed under "Glass."

Professional stained glass artists, studios, and retail dealers will find a wide variety of sand carving related materials such as sand-blast generators, compressors, stencil material, precut die-cut stencils, and design reference books available from the following wholesale suppliers.

Stained Glass Company of New Mexico
4311 Menaul Blvd. N.E.
Albuquerque, NM 87110
505-883-1110

Caters specifically to the needs of the stained glass professional and hobbyist with respect to sand carving equipment. Sponsors classes and seminars introducing sand carving equipment and techniques.

Houston Stained Glass Supply
1829 Arlington
Houston, TX 77008
800-231-0148

D & L Stained Glass Supply
4919 N. Broadway
Boulder, CO 80302
800-525-0940

Ed Hoy's
999 E. Chicago Ave.
Naperville, IL 60540
800-323-5668

Cline Glass Co.
1135 S.E. Grand Ave.
Portland, OR 97214
800-547-8417

Jennifer's Glassworks
P.O. Box 20447
Atlanta, GA 30325
800-241-3388

Porcelain. Retail ceramic suppliers that cater to persons involved in "china painting" or arts/crafts activities related to recreational ceramics. Look in your Yellow Pages under "Arts & Crafts Supplies" or "Ceramics." Plates are the most common items in stock, but persons associated with these businesses will often have the skill and facility to fabricate custom items for you, and can glaze them after carving or sculpturing. You do not want "greenware" that has not yet been high-fired. You want only fine china or porcelain that has been high-fired with a clear glaze for the stencil to adhere to. These dealers will often stock other items such as bells, bowls, and vases that are suitable for sand carving. Also check retail outlets that specialize in import items from the Far East, as many very nice items are made in Japan that are perfect for sand carving.

Professional artists and studios wishing to purchase quantities of materials at wholesale will have to deal directly with ceramics manufacturers or importers.

EQUIPMENT AND SUPPLIES

Compressors, Sand-Blast Generators, Blasting Nozzles, Abrasives, Pressure Regulators, Air Lines, Water/Oil Filters, Exhaust Fans, Dust Collectors, Stencil Materials. For the nonprofessional virtually all of the blasting equipment is available from industrial equipment companies listed in your Yellow Pages. Smaller sized compressors (less than 3 hp) and syphon-feed sand-blast generators or even smaller spray-gun-type setups are available from Sears Department Stores and many well-stocked hardware stores. Stencil materials should be available in small quantities (a few square feet at a time) from local monument makers or stained glass retailers. Small quantities of abrasives are also available from these sources.

If you need very fine abrasives for engraving glassware, try dentists or denture clinics. They are very small blasting cabinets and very fine grits to remove casting investment material from the castings made for dentures, and should sell used abrasives quite inexpensively. Professional sources for abrasives and stencil material will generally have minimum order requirements far in excess of what the occasional user would need; thus, secondary sources tend to save time and money in obtaining the necessary materials for your projects.

Professional users will find all of these materials available from The Stained Glass Company of New Mexico and a number of the other stained glass suppliers listed previously.

Ruemelin Manufacturing Company, Inc. and its distributors specialize in servicing the needs of the abrasive blasting industry, particularly the monument trade. These firms generally have decades of experience in helping the production-oriented facility purchase the finest in state-of-the-art abrasive blasting/handling/recovery systems. For over 60 years Ruemelin Manufacturing Company has been oriented toward constant improvement and field testing of their abrasive systems. Their pressure-pot sand-blast generators are designed with the ultimate in control with respect to airflow/abrasive mix and have an enviable reputation for design innovation, service, and reliability.

The following Ruemelin distributors are well equipped to service the needs of stained glass professionals, glass artists, and studios with equipment that is known as "The Standard of the Industry."

Bicknell Mfg. Co., Inc.
P.O. Box 900
Elberton, GA 30635
800-241-7105

Clearview Equipment Co.
2121 Gravois Ave.
St. Louis, MO 63104
314-776-4500

Dawson-MacDonald Co., Inc.
845 Woburn St.
Wilmington, MA 01887
617-944-4710

Granite City Tool Co.
P.O. Box 368
St. Cloud, MN 56302
800-328-7094

Johnson Granite Supply, Inc.
P.O. Box 12457
North Kansas City, MO 64116
800-821-3488

Leitch and Company, Inc.
971 Howard St.
San Francisco, CA 94103
414-421-8485

George Pfaff, Inc.
16 S. Ketcham
Amityville, NY 11701
516-691-3500

Waldron Company, Inc.
P.O. Box 335
North Haven, CT 06473
203-239-2569

Die-Cut Stencils and Templates. Precut stencils with a wide variety of designs (for the person that does not want to locate resource designs, trace or burnish artwork, and cut the stencil by hand) are available from a number of stained glass suppliers previously listed or through stained glass retailers. Hobbyists and occasional users should anticipate purchasing through your local stained glass retailer.

Wholesale quantities may be available to stained glass professionals through the manufacturer:

Quicksilver Enterprises
Box 3790
San Diego, CA 29103

Custom die-cut stencils are available to glass professionals through:

VM Decal Corporation
9941 York-theta Drive
Cleveland, OH 44133
216-237-0505

All stencils are cut to order with camera-ready art supplied. Pricing will vary with quantity and stencil size.

Custom templates in a variety of materials are available to glass professionals through:

Marvel Marking Products
Mary Jane and S. 30th St.
Pittsburgh, PA 15203
412-381-0700

This company also manufactures "nests" for holding glass articles during etching/engraving and a variety of automatic blasting cabinets for decorating glassware and other small articles. Like die-cut stencils, camera-ready art should be supplied, with pricing varying with stencil material, quantity, and size.

Cutting Blades/Handles, Tracing Paper, Soft Lead Pencils, Dry Transfer Lettering/Designs. All of these materials are available from your local commercial art supply store. Look in the Yellow Pages for "Commercial Art Supplies" or "Artist Supplies." These companies will not be listed under "Arts & Crafts" or any similar heading. Professionals and nonprofessionals should anticipate buying these materials from local sources.

Burnishing Tools (Brayers). These will be available from screen print supply houses, printer supply houses, and retail paint and wallpaper outlets. Look in the Yellow Pages for "Screen Printing Supplies," "Printing Supplies," "Paint," or "Wallpaper." Professionals and nonprofessionals should anticipate buying these materials from local sources.

Denatured Alcohol. This is available from virtually any hardware store or paint store. It is usually sold in pints or gallons. Some dealers will fill your nonglass container for a savings.

Protective Clothing. Such as air-fed hoods, canvas hoods, respirators and gloves. Virtually all distributors of compressors and abrasive blasting equipment will also stock the necessary protective clothing. Other sources may be found in the Yellow Pages under "Fire and Safety Equipment." Distributors for the E.D. Bullard Company (a long-time supplier of safety equipment to the abrasive trade) will also carry a full line of air-fed hoods and support equipment for the professional.

Acid Cream for Screen Printing. Acid creams are manufactured by

McKay Chemical Company
880 Pacific St.
Brooklyn, NY 11238

they are available through its distributors. Many stained glass supply companies also distribute acid cream for glass etching.

An excellent product from Belgium, manufactured by Deca Products of Brussels, is known as "Deca Glassetch" and is distributed by Tube Light, Inc., screen printing suppliers at:

P.O. Box 36067
Charlotte, NC 28236
704-525-2262

or

P.O. Box 07806
Columbus, OH 43207
614-443-9734

This particular acid cream is known for its smoothness of texture and the dense matte surface produced by the powerful acid solution.

Photostates, Film and Paper Positives, Enlargements and Reductions. Available from local typesetting houses or graphic arts companies. Look under "Typesetting" or "Graphic Arts" in the Yellow Pages. Professionals and nonprofessionals should anticipate using the same suppliers.

Impeller Blasters. See the section on Alternative Techniques for a description of the uses of impeller blasters. Models known as "Master Blasters" are available from:

TEXSAW, Inc.
P.O. Box 4668
Waco, TX 76705
817-799-2462

Glossary

This glossary covers virtually all of the terms common to sand carving and many other terms common to the glass trade in general. Many words are included which do not appear in the text of this book, but will be included in other texts that you may come across in your reading about glass. Because many of these other texts assume you are familiar with some basic terminology, and so do not include these words in their glossaries, I have included them for your reference.

abrasive—Any substance used for grinding, cutting, polishing, or sand carving. Useful abrasives include energy Carborundum (silicon carbide), garnet, aluminum oxide, cerium oxide, silica, and pumice. Free-flowing particles are referred to as *grit*.

acid badging—Lightly etching the surface of glass using an acid cream transferred from an engraved metal plate to special transfer tissue for application to the glass. Similar effects can now be obtained through screen printing of acid creams.

acid cut back—A preparation step in traditional cameo carving in which hydrofluoric acid is used to remove all excess glass from the background of the design to be carved in high relief. Typically involves the application of an asphaltum-based acid resist painted on the article to be carved.

acid etching—Chemical erosion of the surface of glass using hydrofluoric-acid solutions. See *French embossing*.

acid polishing—Chemical polishing of glass using hydrofluoric-acid solutions. Typically the piece to be polished is dipped in the solution repeatedly from 10 to 30 seconds, with warm water rinses between dips.

aluminum oxide—The most common abrasive used in sand carving; also known as Alumina.

annealing—The cooling of glass in a controlled manner in order to relieve internal stresses. All glass has an annealing range (temperature) through which it must be cooled evenly. The range will vary with the composition of the glass.

bending—The heating, softening, and sagging of glass in a kiln.

beveled edge—A cut and polished edge on flat glass in the form of an angle or slant; common to mirrors, tabletops, and small shapes for inclusion in stained glass windows.

blank—Any glass article suitable for decoration.

blasting booth—A room used exclusively for sand carving. Booths generally have enough room for the operator to stand inside with the item being worked on. Blasting cabinets are smaller, with the operator standing outside and reaching inside through holes in order to manipulate the blasting nozzle.

bonded glass—Pieces of glass adhered together with resin, glue, or cement.

borosilicate glass—Specially formulated glass used extensively in laboratory ware. Excellent glass for casting. Available as flat glass up to 1 1/4 inch thick.

burnish—To apply or finish by rubbing.

cameo agate—Gemstone material occurring in colored layers which is the inspiration for cameo glass.

cameo glass—A glass object, most often a vase or plate, made up of layers of different colors of glass. The outer layers are cut away resulting in a multicolored, multilayered design in high relief.

camera-ready art—Artwork that is prepared for reproduction through a standard graphic process such as photostating, photo etching, or printing. With respect to artwork necessary for die-cut stencils for glass and photo-etching on glass, the artwork must have no shading or half-tones, only solid black areas or clean whites.

cartoon—Full-sized rendering in pencil of the outline of a design for a stained glass window or sand-carved decoration.

carving—To shape by cutting. With respect to sand carving, the sequential cutting (blasting) of different elements of a design in a way that results in a layered appearance. See also *etching, engraving,* and *sculpturing.*

cased glass—Similar to cameo glass, although generally refers to a single transparent layer (usually ruby or cobalt) added to a clear underlayer.

cathedral glass—A machine-rolled stained glass, usually smooth on one side and textured on the other, and most often 1/8 inch thick.

cerium oxide—Abrasive most used for polishing silica-based gemstone materials. Excellent for optical polishing of glass, particularly lead crystals.

cfm—Cubic feet per minute. See *free air cfm,* and *displacement cfm.*

coefficient of expansion—The degree to which glass expands and contracts during heating and cooling. The c/e must be compatible for glasses being flashed together, blown into cameo blanks, or fused together through sagging.

complex curve—A curve that has the elements of a sphere, as opposed to a simple curve, which has the elements of a cone or cylinder.

compressor—Equipment used to supply air under pressure to a sand-blast generator; made up of an air pump, a pressure tank for storing presurized air, and a motor to power the air pump. Its size is measured in horsepower and free air cubic feet per minute.

copper-wheel engraving—Traditional method of engraving glass dating back to the fifteenth to sixteenth centuries. Based on gemstone engraving or glyptic arts dating back to prehistoric times. Uses finely shaped copper wheels charged with emery or Carborundum spinning on a lathe for abrading the surface of the glass. Quality work requires a very high degree of acquired skill, patience, and sculptural talent.

cords—Optical distortions, similar to currents in water, that appear in glass. High lead glass without cords is very difficult to obtain, particularly for thick objects such as blocks, paperweights, or thick-walled vases.

cullet—Refuse glass suitable for remelting in order to facilitate melting of a glass batch.

curious glass—Odd pieces of stained glass sold as scrap.

cut glass—Generally used to refer to glass

decorated by use of cutting wheels. Designs most common are geometric, facetlike cuts, and stylized florals. Fine figurative renderings would be referred to as wheel engravings. See *copper-wheel engraving*.

dalles—French term for slabs of stained glass varying in thickness from 3/4 to 2 inches and from 8 to 12 inches square. May be used for high-relief carving.

deep cut—A term indicating a depth of cut in an engraving or carving, be it wheel cut or sand carved, that is significant in relation to the thickness of the material that is engraved, or relative to the design that is rendered in glass.

deep "V" cut—The cut obtained when using a V-edged abrasive wheel. See *peaked-out*.

demi-crystal—Clear lead crystal with less than 15 percent lead oxide in the glass batch. Used by Rene Lalique. See also *crystal glass, lead crystal, full lead crystal*.

diamond point engraving—Hand engraving of glass using a diamond-tipped pencillike instrument. Line work and stipple effects are most common.

diamond wheel—Metal wheel impregnated with diamond dust for cutting, shaping, roughing out of wheel-cut engravings, cut glass, and edgework on flat glass.

die-cut stencil—Vinyl-based stencil material incised by a photo-etched plate (die) used to eliminate hand cutting of the stencil.

displacement cfm—A measure of a compressor's ability to deliver air, which is calculated by multiplying the volume of the air pump cylinders by the pump speed measured in rpms. Does not take into account pump efficiency, thus is not as accurate a measure of a compressor's ability to deliver air as is the free air cfm. See *free air cfm*.

double curve—See *complex curve*.

dry transfer lettering/designs—Letter styles and design motifs reproduced on plastic sheets for easy transfer to other surfaces. May be applied to paper in order to obtain camera-ready art, or direct to stencil material for hand cutting.

dsb—Double Strength, B-Grade. Refers to 1/8-inch window pane glass. B-Grade is out of date, as no other grade is currently produced.

dust collector—Equipment used to collect dust resulting from abrasive blasting; may be required by local ordinances covering air pollution.

edge work on flat glass—Refers to the grinding, cutting, and polishing of the edge of 1/4-inch through 3/4-inch flat glass. May be seamed, ground, beveled, double beveled, O.G., pencil, etc. No edge work is termed "clean cut".

engraving—Refers to cutting into the surface of the glass in order to obtain a bas-relief design. Wheel cutting or sand blasting are the most common methods of engraving glass and crystal.

enamelled glass—A vitreous coating applied to the surface of glass for decoration. May be frit based (ground glass powers) or organic lacquer based.

etching—The surface erosion of glass. Chemically it is accomplished by hydrofluoric-acid solutions; physically, by grinding wheels of copper, stone, and diamond and by sand carving.

exhaust fan—A fan installed in a sand-blasting booth or room that creates an air flow used to remove the abrasive dusts.

fire polishing—Polishing of glass by heating it to the point that the surface remelts slightly.

flashed glass—Clear flat glass covered with a thin layer of transparent to translucent colored glass. Most common colors are ruby and cobalt.

flashing—The act of making flashed glass by applying a colored layer of glass to a thin clear layer. See *flashed glass*.

flint glass—An antiquated term for any clear glass.

float plate glass—Flat glass manufactured using a river of molten zinc alloy in order to form a perfectly consistent surface and thickness. It has replaced processes that required polishing of flat glass known as "polished plate" glass.

free air cfm—The measure of the air delivered by a compressor into the atmosphere, measured in cubic feet per minute. It is always stated in relation to a specific pressure. Thus a compressor may be rated at 15.5 free air cfm at 100 psi.

French embossing—A complex procedure of multilevel, multitone acid etching. Requires application or removal of acid resist between multiple acid baths. Different acid solutions are commonly used in order to obtain tonality and texture in the etching.

frit—Finely ground glass; basic material for vitreous enamels to which metal oxides are added as colorants.

frosted glass—Glass having a white, translucent surface. May result from hydrofluoric acid, cutting wheels, or sand blasting.

full lead crystal—Brilliant clear glass containing a minimum of 24 percent lead oxide. A soft glass, excellent for cutting and engraving. Used for the finest glassware, vases, bowls, decanters, etc.

glass decorator—Anyone that in any way alters a glass article after its manufacture, while it is not in a molten state. Includes cutters, engravers, etchers, enamelists, and screen printers. The process is sometimes known as *cold working* because the glass is worked while it is cold (not molten).

glazier—A person who installs glass such as stained glass windows or other architectural glass, ranging from store fronts to window panes.

glazing laws—Federal, state, and local laws that require certain types of flat glass be installed in what are considered hazardous or potentially hazardous situations.

glue chipping—The application of heated animal hide glue to a previously sand-blasted surface in order to obtain an icelike crystalline looking surface. May be single or double chipped, indicating one or two glue treatments.

graphic process (photo process)—As relates to sand-carved glass, it involves the use of a proprietary process in obtaining a stencil through photographic reproductions.

grit—Free-flowing abrasive particles.

hand engraved—All engraving which requires the hand manipulation either of the engraving instrument or the glass article being decorated. Includes all types of wheel engraving, diamond point engraving, and sand carving.

high relief—Engraving, carving, or sculpting any material in such a way that the intended design stands off a cutaway background. See *cameo glass*.

hue—The light tint contained in all clear glass other than fine lead crystal or other water-clear specialty glasses. This tint is very obvious in all float plate glasses and will range from blue, green, and blue-green to yellow or brown. It is most important to match these hues if replacement work is being done where flat glass has been used.

hydrofluoric acid—First produced by C. Sheile, a Swedish chemist, in 1771 by decomposing fluorspar with concentrated sulphuric acid, it is an exceedingly dangerous and powerful acid used in all phases of acid etching on glass, as well as acid polishing. Sand carving offers a safer and easier alternative to many acid-obtained effects.

ices—Frit-based enamels for glass that result in an ice-like crystalline pattern when fired onto the surface of flat glass.

intaglio—An engraved decoration on any hard material that is cut into the surface. It is sometimes accurately described as having the decoration cut below the surface. Opposite of high relief.

kiln—A high-temperature oven used in enameling and sagging/fusing glass.

laminated safety glass—Two sheets of glass bonded together with a clear sheet of plastic. Glazing laws may require it for sand-carved installations in commercial buildings.

lathe—A machine with a rotating spindle to which engraving wheels are attached.

lead crystal—Clear crystal glass that contains lead oxide for added weight and clarity. Less than 15 percent Pbo is termed demicrystal; over

24 percent Pbo is termed full lead crystal. See *crystal glass, full lead crystal.*

lehr (lear, lier)—A tunnellike oven through which glass is moved for annealing.

lumiere—Color rendering of a stained glass window.

luster, metallic—An overglaze, usually reflective, with a metallic base. Includes gold, silver, and platinum lusters.

metallic oxides—Elemental metals combined with oxygen. Used as abrasives, enamel colorants, and glass colorants. Examples include aluminum oxide, cerium oxide, cupric oxide, cobalt oxide, and selenium oxide.

miter cut—Same as V-cut. See *peaked out.*

moisture filter (trap)—Filters used to remove water and oil from air coming out of a compressor tank. Should be placed in the air line prior to the pressure regulator.

mould (mold)—Receptacle used to shape glass by blowing or pressing.

moulded or mould-blown glass (may be molded)—Glass formed by use of a predesigned form called a mould. Generally blown into the mould using man power (mouth blown) or compressed air from compressors. See *pressing.*

multilevel—For engraved, carved, or sculptured glass, it refers to the use of different elevations of cutting in order to obtain the desired bas-relief effects.

nest—A holder used for glassware that is being sand-carved.

nozzle—A tapering spout. With regard to sand carving, it is the controlling element at the end of the blast hose. Most often made of an alumina-based ceramic material.

opalescent glass—A milky, translucent stained glass with swirled colors and white that is often quite brittle and is not particularly good for sand carving.

out of square—A square or rectangle in which the corners are not 90-degree angles. Indicates one or more of the dimensions is too long in relation to the others.

peaked out—In sand carving, a line or element of a design that has been blasted to the point that deep V-cuts or peaks result. Further blasting may result in uncontrolled distortion of the design.

photostat—A high-contrast paper reproduction of any artwork or object made by a graphics art camera. Sometimes referred to as *stats,* these are available from most typesetting houses. They are very useful in adapting reference material into your own original art for sand carving.

plate glass—Formerly used to refer to "polished plate glass" which was rolled then polished on each surface, it currently refers to glass manufactured by the float process and ranging in thickness from 1/4 to 3/4 inch. See *float plate glass.*

point size—The size of lettering. Dry transfer lettering is available only in specific point sizes.

pressed glass—Glass that is placed in a mould and pressed in order to obtain the desired shape. See *moulded* and *mould blown.*

pressure-pot sand-blast generator—The piece of equipment that holds the abrasive grit in a pressurized tank, supplied with air by the compressor. The tank injects the abrasive into the air line, resulting in an abrasive blast coming out of the blast nozzle.

psi—Pounds per square inch, the standard measurement of air pressure.

pyrometer—Temperature gauge for kilns.

refrosted—The etching of parts of a design after line work or other design elements have been engraved or carved.

resist material—Material applied to any substrate which it protects. In the case of the substrate being glass, it may refer to an acid resist or sand-blast resist. Most common sand-blast resists are rubber or vinyl adhesive sheets. See also *templates.*

respirator masks—A mask containing filter materials used to purify dust-filled air for breathing. It is absolutely essential to anyone engaged in sand blasting of any kind.

reverse intaglio—Intaglio decoration on clear or transparent material intended to be viewed through the material.

rock crystal—Semiprecious gemstone material known as quartz. Very suitable for sand blasting.

rondel—Disc of antique stained glass.

sand-blast generator—Equipment used to contain the abrasive used in sand blasting. Air is supplied to the sand-blast generator by the compressor.

sand carving—The etching, engraving, carving, and sculpturing of glass by use of a jet of compressed air and abrasive grit. See *etching, engraving, carving,* and *sculpturing.*

sculptured—Referring to carved glass, this is a further development of carving, in that more form and modeling is given to the rendering of the design. In sand carving, it refers to the individual shaping of the elements making up the stencil breakdown of the design. Also sometimes used by large commercial producers of glass for pressed, mould-blown, or ultrasonically cut glass.

secds—Bubbles in glass.

seedy glass—Flat glass that contains many tiny bubbles resulting in a texture. Not suitable for sand carving.

serif, sans serif—A *serif* is a small projection from the end of a letter. *Sans serif* refers to letters which do not have this feature. Letter styles are classified into one of these two groups.

silica—A mineral consisting of oxygen and silicon. A basic material in glass. Silica dust results from sand blasting either from the glass being blasted or because silica (sand) is used as the abrasive. Inhalation causes silicosis.

silicon carbide—High-quality abrasive used in copper-wheel engraving and sometimes sand carving. Also known as Carborundum.

silicosis—Degenerative lung disease caused by inhaling silica dust. No amount of silica inhalation is considered safe.

slab glass—Transparent stained glass cast in thick slabs for hammer faceting. May be suitable for sand carving.

soda-lime glass—A common glass mixture that contains soda, lime and silica. Decolorizers are often added to reduce the hue from trace elements in the silica. Commonly used for commercial glassware, float plate glass, and art glass.

spindle—The part of the lathe to which cutting wheels are attached. See *lathe* and *copper-wheel engraving.*

ssb—Single Strength, B-Grade. Indicates single-strength window pane flat glass 3/32 inch in thickness. See **dsb.**

stained glass—Glass that is colored with metal oxides or other colorants for use in making stained glass windows or art objects. Will vary greatly in thickness, hardness, transparency, etc., and thus will vary in suitability for sand carving.

stencil breakdown—1. The particular rendering of any design for sand-carving. Any one design will have an unlimited number of stencil breakdowns. 2. The destruction of the resist material (stencil) resulting from overblasting.

stencil material—Any material used as a resist in sand blasting. See *resist material.*

strain point—The lower limit of the temperature range known as the annealing range. See *annealing.*

syphon blaster—Sand-blast generators that depend upon a vacuum resulting from the movement of compressed air past an orifice, and gravity to add abrasive to the air line, resulting in an abrasive blast. Also known as "gravity feed" sand-blast generators. See *pressure-pot sand-blast generators.*

template—Nonadhesive plate made from various materials including brass, plastic, rubber coated metal, etc. Used in etching and engraving glassware, plates, and other decorative accessories in mass production.

tempered glass—Flat glass that has been heat-treated or chemically treated to withstand tremendous blunt shock. Suitable for surface etching only by sand blasting. Widest application is in automotive glass (side lites), shower doors, and sliding glass doors. May be required for commercial installations. See *glazing laws*.

ultrasonic—Used in reference to ultrasonic engraving or sculpturing of glass, it involves the use of ultrasonic sound being translated into linear movement of a metal die which vibrates into the material (glass) being decorated. An abrasive such as silicon carbide is flushed between the die and the glass, thus supplying the cutting action.

vellum—High-quality tracing paper.

vent fan—Exhaust fan.

viscosity—Resistance to flow.

vitreous—Relating to or resembling glass; glasslike. Used in describing materials made of glass or similar to glass; thus, vitreous enamels are glass enamels.

vitrified—Heated and changed into glass or a glasslike consistency.

Index

Index

A

Abels
  Gustov, 131
abrasives, 30
acid cream, 162
acid etching, 159
air pump, 22
art
  camera-ready, 127
  Oriental, 129
art forms, 129

B

Balsamo-Stella
  Guido, 131
Benda
  Eduard, 131
  Jaroslav, 131
  V.H., 131
Biemann
  Dominik, 131
Bittner
  Bob, 6
blades
  cutting, 21
blasting
  basic, 39
blasting nozzles, 30
Bohm

August, 131
Bohnert
  Gertrude, 159
books
  stained glass pattern, 128
border motif on flat glass project, 67, 68
brayer, 22
burnishing tool, 22
butterfly
  carved, 52
  carved and etched, 50
  deep-cut, 50
  engraved line work with solid refrosting, 48
  single-level engraving, 48

C

cabinet
  sand-blasting, 22
Carder
  Frederick, 131
carving, 13, 62
  example of, 50, 52, 62
carving nozzles, 32
centrifugal filter, 29
ceramic plate project, 95
cfm

displacement, 25
  free air, 25
Cigler
  Vaclav, 131
cloison, 130
cloisonne enameling, 130
clothing, 34
  protective, 33
Colette
  Aristide, 131
comparative designs, 46
compressor, 22
  double-stage, 25
  single-stage, 25
compressor head, 22
constant speed control, 26
control
  constant speed, 26
  dual, 26
  pressure switch, 25
copper-wheel engraving
  Czech, 130
  other styles, 131
  Scandinavian, 131
Cristal Lalique, 158
crystal
  full lead, 17
  lead, 17
crystal glass, 17

cutting, 159
Czech copper-wheel engraving, 130

D

decorative accessories, 17
deep cut, 14
deep cutting
    example of, 50, 52, 54, 56
    single-level, example of, 60
deep sculpturing
    example of, 58
design, 22
    tracing the, 38
designs
    comparative, 46
    sources for, 127
    suggested, 104
diamond-point engraving, 159
displacement cfm, 25
double-stage compressor, 25
Drahonosky
    Josef, 131
dual control, 26
dust collector, 30

E

enameling
    cloisonne, 130
Engelhard
    David, 130
engraved line work
    example of, 48
engraving, 13, 159
    Czech copper-wheel, 130
    diamond-point, 159
    example of, 56
    high-relief, 39
    reverse intaglio, 39
    single-level, example of, 60
    ultrasonic, 162
equipment
    access to, 41
etching, 13
    acid, 160
    laser, 164
exercises for the novice glass
        sculptor, 137
exhaust fan, 30

F

filter
    centrifugal, 29
    oil, 29
    water, 29
flat glass, 15
    problems with, 44
fleur-de-lis
    deep-cut, 52
    deep-cut, refrosted, 56
    deep-cut, solid refrosted, shaded
        refrosted, 54
    deep-cut and etched, 54

floral motif on flat glass project, 139
free air cubic feet per minute, 25
Freres
    Muller, 131
Fritche
    William, 131
full lead crystal, 17
further study
    sources for, 127

G

Galle
    Emile, 131
Gate
    Simon, 131
generators
    sand-blast, 26
glass
    pressed or molded, 158
    sand-carved, 1
glass cleaner, 22
glass rack, 35
glassware
    problems with, 42
Gottstein
    Franz, 131
Greenwood
    Franz, 160

H

Hald
    Edvard, 131
Hansel
    Franz, 131
Harcuba
    Jiri, 131
head gear
    protective, 33
health hints, 45
helmet
    air-fed, 33
high-relief, 12
high-relief bud vase project, 144
high-relief engraving, 39
Hill
    Oliver, 5
history of sand-carved glass, 1
Hlava
    Pavel, 131
Hodgetts
    Joshua, 131
Hoffman
    Emanuel, 131
Horejc
    Haroslav, 131
horsepower, 26
hp, 26

I

impeller blasting, 158
Ingrand
    Max, 5

intaglio, 12
    reverse, 12, 39
intaglio and high-relief combination
        project, 68
intercooler, 25

J

Jeannin
    Gaetan, 5

K

Kepka Brothers, 7
Kretschman
    F., 131
Kysela
    Frantisek, 131

L

laser etching, 164
lead crystal, 17
Lehman
    Caspar, 130
lighting, 35
Lindstrand
    Vicke, 131
Liskova
    Vera, 131
Lobmeyr
    J., 131
    L., 131
Locke
    Joseph, 131
Luce
    Jean, 5

M

material
    stencil, 20
material to be decorated, 20
materials, 47
    assorted, 35
Mattoni
    A.H., 131
Meadows
    William, 160
measuring tape
    steel, 35
Michel
    Eugene, 131
mold blown, 158
molded glass, 158
monogrammed glassware and
        decanter project, 67, 74
motor, 24
multilevel engraved and etched
        plate project, 67
multilevel engraving/etching project,
        86

N

NIOSH approved, 34
novice glass sculptor

exercises for, 137
nozzles
  blasting, 30
  carving, 32
  shaping, 32

O

oil filter, 29
Oliva
  Ladislav, 7
  Ladislov, 131
opaque projector, 36
Oriental art, 129
Orrefors Glasbruk, 131
overblast, 43
overhead projector, 36
Owens-Illinois Glass Company, 158

P

pantograph, 36
paper
  tracing, 21
paper positives, 140
pattern books
  stained glass, 128
Peace
  D.B., 160
Pelikan
  F.A., 131
pencil, 22
Perlman
  Herman, 6
Pfeiffer
  A.H., 131
Pfofl
  Karl, 131
photostats, 140
Pogue
  Ivan, 6
Pollitzer
  Sigmund, 5
porcelain plate project, 95
Prenosil
  Ladislav, 131
pressed glass, 158
pressure regulator, 29
pressure switch control, 25
pressure tank, 24
project
  border motif on flat glass, 67, 68
  floral motif on flat glass, 139
  high-relief bud vase, 144
  intaglio and high-relief combina-
    tion, 68
  monogrammed glassware and
    decanter, 67, 74
  multilevel engraved and etched
    plate, 67
  multilevel engraving/etching, 86

porcelain plate, 95
sculptured porcelain plate, 150
projector
  opaque, 36
  overhead, 36
projects
  advanced, 136

R

reference materials, 36
refrosting
  example of, 56
  solid, 48
regulator
  pressure, 29
relief, 7
resists
  sand-blast, 21
  screen-printed, 157
respirator mask, 34
reverse intaglio, 12
reverse intaglio engraving, 39
rooster
  deep-sculptured, 58
  engraved and refrosted, 56
  sculptured and etched, 58
rose
  carved, 62
  engraved or deep-cut, 60
  etched, 60
Roubicek
  Rene, 131
Rousseau
  F.E., 131
Rozsypal
  Ivo, 131
rpm, 25

S

sand-blast generator, 26
sand-blast resists, 21
sand-blasting cabinet, 22
sand-carved glass, 1
  history of, 1
  process of, 7
Scandinavian copper-wheel engraving, 131
Schindler
  George, 130
Schwanhardt
  George the Elder, 130
screen-printed resists, 157
sculptural fullness, 54
sculptured porcelain plate project,
  150
sculpturing, 13
shaded etching
  example of, 50, 58, 60
shaded refrosting

example of, 54
shaping nozzles, 32
single-level engraving
  example of, 48
single-phase motor, 26
single-stage compressor, 25
solid etching
  example of, 54
solid refrosting
  example of, 48, 54, 56
Sources
  books, 132
sources for designs and further
  study, 127
stage blasting, 13
stained glass pattern books, 128
stats, 140
stencil, 7, 8
stencil cutting, 38
stencil material, 20
straightedge, 35
suit
  air-fed, 33

T

table, 35
techniques
  alternative, 157
tempered glass, 15
template, 7
Thorpe
  Dorothy, 5
towel, 22
tracing paper, 21
tracing the design, 38
trap, 29
triple-phase motor, 26

U

ultrasonic engraving, 162
utility light, 36

V

Von Eiff
  Wilhelm, 131

W

wheel cutting, 159
Whistler
  Lawrence, 160
Wilson
  H. Warren, 160
  W.J., 160
Winter
  Friedrich, 130
water filter, 29
Wolff
  David, 160

Other Bestsellers of Related Interest

YEAR-ROUND CRAFTS FOR KIDS
—Barbara L. Dondiego, Illustrated by Jacqueline Cawley

Easy to use, the handy month-by-month format provides a year of inspiring projects, many focused on seasonal themes to ensure young children's enthusiasm. Valentines, paper airplanes, and cookies for Easter, paper bag bunny puppets, string painting, Hanukkah candles and gingerbread boys, bell and candle mobiles and of course Christmas trees for December are just a few of the fun things to make. 256 pages, 180 illustrations, plus 8 color pages. Book No. 2904, $14.95 paperback only

ME TOO! Creative Crafts for Preschoolers
—Sarah H. Healton, Ed.D. and Kay Healton Whiteside

Assist children ages 3 to 5 with developmental challenges. This book provides indispensable guidance by helping you match specific projects to the unique educational levels and needs of the children in your life. The projects assembled here are accompanied by a special chart indicating which activities are most useful for improving muscle development, eye-hand coordination, memory and sequence recognition, left/right concept, communication skills, math and reading readiness, and the ability to follow directions. 112 pages, 173 two-color illustrations. Book No. 4183, $9.95 paperback, $16.95 hardcover

Kathy Lamancusa's Guide to GREAT IDEAS FOR GIFT BASKETS, BAGS, AND BOXES
—Kathy Lamancusa

Capitalize on the booming gift basket industry with unique gift baskets designed especially for the recipient. The book will get you started by showing you creative ways to use materials—including bows, ribbons, and balloons. Then a series of original, step-by-step projects shows you how to add individual touches while focusing on specific themes: bon voyage, birthday, anniversary, I-love-you, holidays, household decoration, and much more. 152 pages, 95 illustrations, 8-full color pages. Book No. 3899, $12.95 paperback only

WEARABLE ART—Kathy Lamancusa, C.P.D.

Create fantastic decorative clothing with this ultimate instruction and idea book. It provides all the necessary information for making wearables, and examines basic techniques and types of embellishments. 128 pages, 190 illustrations, 8-page color section. Book No. 3900, $10.95 paperback only

CRAFTS FOR KIDS: A Month-by-Month Idea Book—Barbara L. Dondiego

Creative and educational crafts for small children designed by a professional! More than 160 craft and cooking projects that can be made easily and inexpensively, from readily available materials! Step-by-step instructions plus exceptional illustrations enhance projects which are arranged by months to take advantage of special seasonal occasions! 224 pages, 156 illustrations. Book No. 1784, $11.95 paperback, $17.95 hardcover

MAKING POTPOURRI, COLOGNES AND SOAPS—102 NATURAL RECIPES David A. Webb

Fill your home with the scents of spring—all year long! This down-to-earth guide reintroduces the almost forgotten art of home crafts. You'll learn how to use simple ingredients (flowers, fruits, spices, and herbs) to make a variety of useful scented products, from soaps and deodorant to potpourris and colognes. Webb demystifies this age-old craft and offers step-by-step diagrams, work-in-progress photographs, and easy-to-follow recipes to give you everything you need to successfully create your own home crafts. 144 pages, 98 illustrations. Book No. 2918, $10.95 paperback, $18.95 hardcover

STRIP QUILTING—Diane Wold

Diane Wold is an expert quilt-maker and her enthusiasm for the art of strip quilting is contagious. After introducing you to the tools, fabrics, techniques, and sewing methods used in strip quilting, she covers all the steps needed to complete a finished project including making borders, backing, using batting, basting, doing the actual quilting, and binding. You'll also find directions for using different types of patterns—multiple bands, on-band shifted patterns, and more. 184 pages, 165 illustrations, with 8 color pages. Book No. 2822, $24.95 paperback only

SELLING WHAT YOU MAKE: Profit from Your Handcrafts—James E. Seitz, Ph.D.

This book focuses on reaching your business goals through methods that have proven successful in retail stores, in-home shops, craft shows and bazaars, and—especially—through the home-party method. It covers planning your start-up in detail, plus such nuts-and-bolts issues as permits, taxes, recordkeeping, and pricing, so you can establish your enterprise quickly and without the help of high-priced attorneys and consultants. 224 pages, 32 illustrations. Book No. 4235, $12.95 paperback only

FRAMES AND FRAMING:
The Ultimate Illustrated How-to-Do-It-Guide
—Gerald F. Laird and Louise Meiere Dunn, CPF

This illustrated step-by-step guide gives complete instructions and helpful illustrations on how to cut mats, choose materials, and achieve attractively framed art. Filled with photographs and eight pages of full color, this book shows why a frame's purpose is to enhance, support, and protect the artwork, and never call attention to itself. You can learn how to make a beautiful frame that complements artwork. 208 pages, 264 illustrations, 8 color pages. Book No. 2909, $15.95 paperback only

AFTER-SCHOOL CRAFTS—Barbara L. Dondiego, Illustrations by Jacqueline Cawley

Spend quality time with your kids and these fun and educational projects. This collection of projects involves kids ages 6 to 12 in cooking, painting, molding clay, cutting, drawing, pasting, and writing. It also teaches the use of colors, shapes, numbers, letters, language, and other essentials. Projects include coffee filter snowflakes, a baby food jiggle jar, a shoebox Valentine and a variety of Christmas decorations. 148 pages, 100 illustrations, 4-page full-color insert. Book No. 4138, $12.95 paperback only

Prices Subject to Change Without Notice.

Look for These and Other TAB Books at Your Local Bookstore

To Order Call Toll Free 1-800-822-8158
(24-hour telephone service available.)

or write to TAB Books, Blue Ridge Summit, PA 17294-0840.

Title	Product No.	Quantity	Price

☐ Check or money order made payable to TAB Books

Charge my ☐ VISA ☐ MasterCard ☐ American Express

Acct. No. _____ Exp. _____

Signature: _____

Name: _____

Address: _____

City: _____

State: _____ Zip: _____

Subtotal	$ _____
Postage and Handling ($3.00 in U.S., $5.00 outside U.S.)	$ _____
Add applicable state and local sales tax	$ _____
TOTAL	$ _____

TAB Books catalog free with purchase; otherwise send $1.00 in check or money order and receive $1.00 credit on your next purchase.

Orders outside U.S. must pay with international money in U.S. dollars drawn on a U.S. bank.

TAB Guarantee: If for any reason you are not satisfied with the book(s) you order, simply return it (them) within 15 days and receive a full refund.

BC